AIMR Conference Proceedings
Practical Issues in Equity Analysis

Presentations selected from the following AIMR seminars:

"Financial Analysts Seminar–Asia"
October 21–22, 1998
Hong Kong

"Equity Research and Valuation Techniques"
December 8, 1998
Philadelphia, Pennsylvania

"Investing Worldwide X"
February 1–3, 1999
San Francisco, California

"Global Investment Strategy"
(11th SAAJ–AIMR Joint Seminar)
March 1–3, 1999
Kisarazu, Japan

"Using Behavioral Finance to Improve Investment Decisions"
March 16, 1999
Philadelphia, Pennsylvania

Association for Investment Management and Research

Dedicated to the Highest Standards of Ethics, Education, and Professional
Practice in Investment Management and Research.

To obtain the *AIMR Publications Catalog*, contact:
AIMR, 560 Ray C. Hunt Drive, Charlottesville, Virginia 22903, U.S.A.
Phone 804-951-5499; Fax 804-951-5262; E-mail info@aimr.org
or
visit AIMR's World Wide Web site at www.aimr.org
to view the AIMR publications list.

CFA®, CHARTERED FINANCIAL ANALYST™, AIMR-PPS™, GIPS™, and Financial Analysts Journal® are just a few of the trademarks owned by the Association for Investment Management and Research. To view a list of the Association for Investment Management and Research's trademarks and a Guide for the Use of AIMR's Marks, please visit our Web site at www.aimr.org.

©2000, Association for Investment Management and Research

All rights reserved. No part of this publication may be reproduced, stored in a retrieval system, or transmitted, in any form or by any means, electronic, mechanical, photocopying, recording, or otherwise, without prior written permission of the copyright holder.

AIMR Conference Proceedings (ISSN 1086-5055; USPS 013-739) is published four times a year in June, August, August, and December by the Association for Investment Management and Research, 560 Ray C. Hunt Drive, Charlottesville, Virginia 22903, U.S.A. This publication is designed to provide accurate and authoritative information with regard to the subject matter covered. It is sold with the understanding that the publisher is not engaged in rendering legal, accounting, or other professional services. If legal advice or other expert assistance is required, the services of a competent professional should be sought. Periodicals postage paid at the post office in Richmond, Virginia, and additional mailing offices.

Copies are mailed as a benefit of membership to CFA® charterholders. Subscriptions also are available at US$100 for one year. Address all circulation communications to AIMR Conference Proceedings, 560 Ray C. Hunt Drive, Charlottesville, Virginia 22903, U.S.A.; Phone 804-951-5499; Fax 804-951-5262. For change of address, send mailing label and new address six weeks in advance.

Postmaster: Send address changes to the Association for Investment Management and Research, P.O. Box 3668, Charlottesville, Virginia 22903.

ISBN 0-935015-45-0
Printed in the United States of America
February 2000

Editorial Staff

Roger S. Mitchell
Editor

Jaynee M. Dudley
Production Manager

Fiona D. Russell Cowen
Assistant Editor

Cheryl Likness
Production Coordinator

Lois A. Carrier
Composition

Contents

Foreword iv
    Katrina F. Sherrerd, CFA

Biographies v

Overview: Practical Issues in Equity Analysis 1
    Jan R. Squires, CFA

Value Enhancement and Valuation Models 4
    Aswath Damodaran

Financial Reporting and Disclosure for Equity Analysis 18
    Paul R. Brown

Cross-Border Financial Statement Analysis 27
    Gary S. Schieneman

Old and New Perspectives on Equity Risk 37
    Philip S. Fortuna

The Value Added by Equity Analysts 46
    Kent L. Womack

Investor Overreaction and Contrarian Strategies 55
    David N. Dreman

Global Equity Management and Valuation 65
    M. Campbell Gunn

Valuing Zero-Income Stocks: A Practical Approach 75
    Barney Wilson

Analyzing Asian Companies 83
    Richard H. Lawrence, Jr., CFA

References 92

Selected Publications 95

Foreword

Equity analysis has a way of being both cutting edge and conservative at the same time. Although investors are constantly adapting their approaches to evolving market conditions, many of the fundamental tenets of equity analysis have remained virtually unchanged since the work of Benjamin Graham in the 1930s and 1940s and the development of modern portfolio theory in the 1950s. The unprecedented challenges faced by today's equity analysts, however, demand innovation.

But innovation does not necessarily require a complete overhaul of established methodology. The presentations in *Practical Issues in Equity Analysis* show that, although the problems confronted by equity analysts may be as tricky as adjusting for cross-border accounting differences and determining the right valuation for Internet companies that have no earnings but extraordinary market capitalizations, the solution may be as straightforward as modifying familiar methods to account for new circumstances. In other cases, revisiting the historical and theoretical underpinnings of a widely used tool, such as standard deviation in risk measurement, can make a new approach seem like a logical extension rather than a radical departure.

The presentations in this proceedings were given at four AIMR seminars and were selected for publication because they share a focus on current issues in equity analysis. The authors have different professional backgrounds and draw on a variety of approaches, from behavioral finance to measurement theory to basic industry analysis, but they are alike in concentrating on the real-world implications of their insights. Together, the presentations provide an overview of today's challenges in equity analysis that is both eminently practical and theoretically provocative.

We wish to extend our thanks to the speakers for their valuable contributions: From "Financial Analysts Semiar–Asia"—Richard H. Lawrence, Jr., CFA, Overlook Investments Ltd. From "Equity Research and Valuation Techniques"—Paul Brown, New York University; Aswath Damodaran, New York University; Barney Wilson, Putnam Investments. From "Investing Worldwide X"—Gary S. Schieneman, Merrill Lynch & Company. From "Global Investment Strategy" (11th SAAJ–AIMR Joint Seminar)—M. Campbell Gunn, Meiji Dresdner Asset Management. From "Using Behavioral Finance to Improve Investment Decisions"—David Dreman, Dreman Value Management; Philip S. Fortuna, Scudder Kemper Investments; Kent L. Womack, Dartmouth College.

Katrina F. Sherrerd, CFA
Senior Vice President
Educational Products

Biographies

Paul R. Brown is chair of the department of Accounting, Taxation, and Business Law at New York University's Stern School of Business. He has also worked as an auditor for Arthur Andersen & Company and as a staff member of the Financial Accounting Standards Board. He is the founding editor-in-chief of the *Journal of Financial Statement Analysis*. Professor Brown is a member of both the American Institute of Certified Public Accountants and the American Accounting Association. He received his doctoral degree from the University of Texas at Austin.

Aswath Damodaran is associate professor of finance at the New York University Stern School of Business. Previously, he served as a visiting professor at the University of California at Berkeley. In 1994, *Business Week* magazine selected Professor Damodaran as one of the top 12 business school professors in the United States. He has published numerous articles and authored several books on equity valuation and corporate finance. Professor Damodaran holds an M.B.A. and a Ph.D. from the University of California at Los Angeles.

David N. Dreman is chair, chief investment officer, and founder of Dreman Value Management, L.L.C. In his 20-year career as an investment advisor and security analyst, Mr. Dreman has served as director of New York research for Rauscher Pierce Refsnes Securities Corporation, as senior investment officer with J.&W. Seligman & Company, and as a senior editor with the Value Line Investment Office. He has authored a number of books, including *Contrarian Investment Strategies: The Next Generation*, and has published articles in various finance journals.

Philip S. Fortuna is a managing director of Scudder Kemper Investments, where he is director of the quantitative group. Previously, Mr. Fortuna was director of investment operations, director of quantitative services, and an institutional portfolio manager. Prior to joining Scudder, he served as a strategic planning officer for Crocker National Corporation and as an investment officer for Crocker Investment Management Corporation. Mr. Fortuna holds a B.S. in economics from Carnegie Mellon University and an M.B.A. from the University of Chicago.

M. Campbell Gunn is chief investment officer, Japan, of Meiji Dresdner Asset Management, a joint-venture company of Dresdner RCM. He was previously chief investment officer, Asia, of Dresdner RCM and has served as a member of a New York hedge fund group specializing in Asian equities, as managing director at Goldman Sachs Asset Management, and as director of Banque Kleinwort Benson SA Geneva. Mr. Gunn holds a B.A. in Jurisprudence from New College, Oxford, and is a Barrister of Law of the Inner Temple.

Richard H. Lawrence, Jr., CFA, is chair and managing director for Overlook Investments Limited, where he serves as chief investment officer for The Overlook Partners Fund LP, a limited partnership founded in 1992 to invest in publicly listed Asian equities. Previously, he served as vice president of F.P. Special Assets Ltd. and vice president of J. Bush & Company. Mr. Lawrence holds a B.A. in economics from Brown University.

Gary S. Schieneman is a vice president responsible for comparative global equity analysis at Merrill Lynch & Company. His work is sector oriented and identifies appropriate financial criteria for comparing companies on a cross-border basis. Mr. Schieneman also worked as director of Latin American research and as the Latin American strategist at Smith New Court and as a global accounting analyst with Prudential Securities, where he identified and explained accounting issues that affect comparative market and specific company valuation. Previously, Mr. Schieneman was a C.P.A. and partner in the International Service Group at Arthur Young, where he served as the expert on international accounting issues.

Barney Wilson is an equity research analyst and vice president at Putnam Investments; he is a technology and beverage analyst in global equity research. Prior to joining Putnam, Mr. Wilson worked in corporate finance at Robertson, Stephens & Company, where he focused on technology companies. Mr. Wilson holds a B.A. in mathematics from the University of Virginia, a J.D. from the University of Virginia School of Law, and an M.B.A. from the Haas School of Business, University of California at Berkeley.

Kent L. Womack is associate professor of finance at the Amos Tuck School of Business Administration at Dartmouth College. His research interests focus on the value of security analysis, security analysts' conflicts of interest, and the underwriting of initial public offerings. Some of his recent studies have been published in the *Journal of Finance*, the *Wall Street Journal*, and the *Economist*. Professor Womack holds a Ph.D. in finance from the Johnson Graduate School of Management at Cornell University, a B.A. in economics and mathematics from Yale University, and an M.B.A. from the Graduate School of Business at Stanford University.

Overview: Practical Issues in Equity Analysis

Jan R. Squires, CFA
Vice President
AIMR

From time to time, even such a widely accepted and intensively applied discipline as equity analysis can benefit from a fresh look at the content of its practice and the insights of its most accomplished practitioners. The pace of change in the global equity markets—the speed with which new technologies appear and then become obsolete, the rapidity and ferocity with which financial distresses appear, the accelerated introduction of new instruments and abolition of old barriers—makes such a review all the more compelling. Merely the acronyms encountered in modern equity analysis pose a formidable learning unit: P/E (price/earnings), EV/EBITDA (enterprise value/earnings before interest, taxes, depreciation, and amortization), EVA (economic value added), MVA (market value added), SVA (shareholder value added), ROI (return on investment), and CFROI (cash flow return on investment) are only a sample. Mastering the nuances of the underlying models requires both revisiting the old fundamentals and recognizing the new frontiers.

The presentations in this proceedings have been selected from five AIMR seminars because they share themes related to sharpening the current vision of equity analysis and expanding the set of practical analytical tools. The authors compose an eclectic blend of practitioners and academics, whose shared characteristic is an uncanny ability to integrate the best of traditional insights with cutting-edge concepts necessitated by the complexity of today's (never mind tomorrow's) global equity environment.

This proceedings addresses practical issues in equity analysis from three perspectives:
- *Tools:* What is the real nature of the "new" value enhancement and valuation paradigms? What is the proper focus of financial analysis in the modern equity environment? What are the challenges and implications of cross-border financial analysis? Are traditional risk measures adequate and appropriate?
- *General issues:* What value is added by professional equity analysts? What are the nature and consequences of investor overreaction in the equity markets? What should be the basis for structuring and valuing global equity portfolios?
- *Specific applications:* How should equity analysts view zero-income stocks, emerging market securities, and Asian companies?

Tools

Aswath Damodaran begins the discussion of equity analysis tools by engaging readers in a wide-ranging exploration of issues inherent in value enhancement and valuation models. He points out that the supposedly "new" value enhancement tools—EVA, CFROI, and the like—are in reality deeply rooted in traditional discounted cash flow (DCF) valuation and thus not new at all. As such, they share many of the same estimation difficulties (e.g., cash flows, growth rates, and risk premiums, to name just a few). To demonstrate the kinds of advances necessary to justify describing a model as "new," Damodaran illustrates alternative approaches for estimating equity risk premiums and for modifying regression-generated beta factors. He then turns his attention to value creation, identifying four paths to value creation, contrasting these paths with value-neutral actions that companies often take, and specifying what he terms the "value enhancement chain." He takes time to examine in detail—and suggest adjustments and precautions for using—EVA. To illustrate the similarities in old and "new" valuation models, Damodaran closes by providing a valuation example using both EVA and DCF approaches.

In the face of an increasingly complex environment in which companies routinely report no profits or revenues and are driven mostly by human capital and technology, Paul Brown argues that equity analysts need information in a type and form not typically imparted by traditional financial reporting and disclosure models. He describes a five-step model for obtaining such information. He discusses in detail the first three steps of the model, which demand uncompromising attention to detail and due diligence, and Brown contends that any analyst who attempts to reach conclusions with respect to profitability, risk, and value without undertaking these steps is at a real loss, especially in the many cases in which industry and company assets are not captured on the balance sheet. He emphasizes that identifying economic characteristics and company strategies is best accomplished at the product level. He also uses several

©2000, Association for Investment Management and Research

company examples to illustrate the pitfalls that arise from earnings management and that can be uncovered by the process of "cleansing" the financial statements. Brown closes his discussion with an in-depth look at disclosures (or the lack thereof) for research and development activities and costs.

Gary Schieneman continues the discussion of financial statement analysis by focusing on how accounting differences among countries affect the way analysts look at companies and markets. He begins with four telling observations about the current "state of the art" in accounting and the implications for analysis and for investment decision making. Schieneman then turns his attention to the effects of cross-border accounting differences on company analysis and uses three case studies to illustrate different treatments of goodwill and other accounting items. Similarly, he examines the impact, for several markets, of accounting differences on valuation-specific measures, particularly market multiples and reported earnings; in addition, he uses the German and Japanese markets to explore the importance of tax considerations in the valuation process. Accounting differences also affect traditional valuation models, and Schieneman takes readers through a consideration of several such models—from P/E to EVA—in a cross-border context. He concludes that global financial analysis is difficult if not impossible without making appropriate adjustments for cross-border accounting differences and, although differences are shrinking, greater harmonization is still needed.

Because insufficient attention has been paid to measuring, defining, and assessing investment risk, argues Philip Fortuna, many if not most investment professionals are using misspecified risk measures. Building on the traditional investment risk framework developed by Harry Markowitz, Fortuna introduces concepts of measurement theory—validity, reliability, and utility—to compare the variance measure with less traditional lower-partial-moment measures of risk—downside frequency, average downside, and semivariance—which share a common focus on the individual's risk threshold. Fortuna draws on insights from psychology, investment management, and public behavior to estimate the validity of the risk measures; examines mutual fund returns to form reliability conclusions; and focuses on variance versus semivariance to address utility. In a test of how the risk measures performed in asset allocation between Japanese and U.S. equities, Fortuna found that a downside-risk optimized portfolio generated superior performance compared with mean-variance optimized and naively constructed portfolios. He concludes by admonishing analysts to consider using downside measures of risk, which are valid, reliable, and relatively easy to calculate.

General Issues

Kent Womack's contribution to the discussion of general issues of equity analysis is an unflinching empirical assessment of the performance of equity analysts in three key tasks: forecasting earnings, making securities recommendations, and helping sell new securities. A review of financial research suggests that equity analysts' performance in forecasting earnings is, to use Womack's characterization, "mediocre to bad." His own research on analysts' recommendations reveals substantial differences in magnitude and duration of value among three types of recommendations—new buys, new sells, and removals from buy. Womack's research also indicates that analysts tend to focus on different fundamental factors in support of different types of recommendations and that buy recommendations based on "new initiatives" are more valuable than those based on "attractive valuation." With respect to the sale of new securities, Womack finds strong evidence to suggest that underwriter-affiliated analysts behave quite differently from unaffiliated analysts, with significantly different performance implications and with the potential for serious conflicts of interest. He concludes by suggesting four simple heuristics that investors should use in dealing with equity analysts' information and recommendations.

David Dreman guides readers through much of the extensive research literature that explores the controversial phenomenon of investor overreaction—controversial, that is, because if markets are efficient, investors should not overreact—in equity markets. His discussion explores whether overreaction actually occurs and, if so, when and why; includes evidence about the performance of the contrarian strategies designed to take advantage of such behavior; and attempts to reconcile over- and underreaction. Dreman says that overreaction and underreaction are part of the same process and are distinguished essentially by whether they occur at, before, or after portfolio formation. Both behaviors, he argues, are part of the ebb and flow of market returns, and both are catalysts for market bubbles and panics, of which he provides recent examples and identifies three alternative explanations. Dreman believes that contrarian equity investing strategies work because investors, by making cognitive and other psychological errors, move away from fundamental valuation factors. He contends that the extensive body of research on this phenomenon supports at least four important conclusions for investors to keep in mind to either take advantage of underreaction or avoid overreaction.

Campbell Gunn concludes the discussion of general issues in equity analysis by exploring two questions critical to all global equity investors: the basis for portfolio construction and the choice of valuation method. The traditional approach to global equity portfolio construction—and, consequently, to the organization of the investment management firm—has been based in macroeconomic analysis, taking a top-down view and emphasizing country selection. Gunn contends, however, that such an approach has major drawbacks, and his organization takes a different approach, one that emphasizes global sectors and local markets within a predominantly bottom-up perspective. Emphasizing sector analysis, however, also exposes the limitations of traditional valuation approaches. Gunn provides "scorecards" that compare the requirements for using three traditional valuation methods—P/E, EV/EBITDA, ROI—and three alternative methods—EVA, SVA, CFROI. He then uses Toyota Motor Corporation and Microsoft Corporation as case studies to compare what he believes to be the two strongest of the six valuation alternatives, and he concludes with suggestions about how best to implement any new valuation methodologies.

Specific Applications

Barney Wilson shifts the focus of the proceedings to specific equity analysis applications by addressing the challenges of valuing zero-income stocks. He first establishes the importance of having a view on such stocks; the lack of a view ignores securities that are increasingly entering the investment mainstream, with larger and larger capitalizations, and exposes the analyst to potentially serious confusion in the face of the price behavior of such stocks. Wilson then recounts the problems encountered in applying traditional present-value-based methodologies to zero-income stocks—dealing with a wide range of critical inputs, finding the right discount rate, and estimating the proper "fade rate" to characterize changes in expected growth. To address these problems, he proposes several adjustments to traditional PV-based methodologies, adjustments that encompass differing growth rates, multiple expected value scenarios, and factors to supplement the basic DCF model. In conclusion, Wilson stresses that valuing zero-income stocks requires not only adjustments of technique but also a change in analytical focus and a willingness to go beyond the notion of a single "fair value" for a stock.

Richard Lawrence concludes the discussion of specific applications by sharing the tools, practices, and experiences of a Hong Kong-based investment firm that specializes in analyzing Asian companies. The approaches espoused by Lawrence are rooted in the fundamental analysis of Benjamin Graham and David Dodd and built on a foundation that recognizes five different definitions of cash flow. Equity analysis inevitably involves projections of earnings and other variables, and Lawrence details four general principles to keep in mind in preparing such projections. He also introduces the concept of an "earnings digest," which can impart a discipline and process for effective monitoring of portfolio characteristics and performance. He next proceeds to a discussion of specific valuation approaches, including ratios based on enterprise value and a method he calls "get close to cash." Lawrence concludes with a number of practical checklists for equity analysis in the Asian markets—the characteristics of successful Asian managers; the many ways in which value has been destroyed, especially for minority shareholders, in Asian markets; and the success factors in Asian investing.

Conclusion

Although valuation in current and future equity markets may seem daunting, these authors convey a clear and somewhat comforting message: Equity analysis is still relevant and may be made even more so. Their lessons are straightforward: What equity investors need is a continual renewing of fundamental tenets—careful use of information, substantive financial analysis, appropriate risk measurement, and meaningful valuation models—combined with a keen eye for the requirements of specific analytical situations and an honest recognition of the realities of a truly global investment environment.

Value Enhancement and Cash-Driven Valuation Models

Aswath Damodaran
Associate Professor of Finance
New York University Stern School of Business

> Because the "new" value enhancement tools, such as EVA, are simply derivatives of the traditional discounted cash flow model, they offer no truly new advances. When used for valuation, these value enhancement methods also present the same core challenges of estimation as DCF analysis, such as cash flows, growth rates, and risk premiums. The key to effective valuation remains unchanged: choosing the right methods for estimating critical variables and understanding the real nature of value creation.

In the past 10 years, value enhancement has become the mantra of consultants and investment banks, who recognize that this concept is a cash cow. As a result, various new measures for value enhancement, such as economic value added (EVA), have come into existence.

This presentation attempts to put the concept of value enhancement in perspective by providing an appreciation of the underlying principles of cash-driven valuation models. The first section examines the basic aspects of the discounted cash flow (DCF) model and reconsiders some of the fundamental estimation issues that typically cause problems in this type of analysis. The second section analyzes the limited number of ways in which companies can truly create value and explains how investors can distinguish between value-neutral actions and value-enhancing actions. The third section directly evaluates the most prominent value enhancement concept, EVA, and compares it with DCF analysis

Discounted Cash Flow and Estimates

The value of an asset, in a DCF approach, is the present value of the expected cash flows from that asset. The cornerstone equation of DCF analysis is

$$\text{Value} = \sum_{t=1}^{t=n} \frac{CF_t}{(1+r)^t},$$

where
- n = life of the asset
- CF_t = cash flow in period t
- r = discount rate reflecting the riskiness of the estimated cash flows

We can debate whether anyone can estimate these cash flows correctly or get the discount rate right, but we should not be debating whether, in fact, this equation is correct. The equation is not a hypothesis; it is always true.

To perform DCF valuation, we start with the after-tax operating income and subtract reinvestment needs. The result is the cash flow before debt payments but after reinvestments, called the free cash flow to the company. Next, we make a projection that cash flows will grow at some rate. Fundamentally, this growth rate has to be a function of two things—how much is reinvested and how well it is reinvested. The reinvestment rate times the return on capital (or the return on invested capital) provides the expected growth rate.

The problem in valuing a company, unlike valuing a finite-life asset, is that companies theoretically have infinite life, but cash flows cannot be projected forever. To get closure, we assume that at some point in the future the company's cash flows will grow at a constant rate; this growth rate has to be less than or equal to the growth rate of the economy in which the company operates. This assumption allows us to estimate the terminal value at that point. Using exit multiples to get the terminal value is not a part of DCF valuation; it converts the analysis to a relative valuation.

Estimating when the growth rate in cash flows will be less than or equal to the growth rate of cash flows and earnings in the entire economy is a challenge faced in every DCF valuation, and investors should give more thought to this issue. The length of the high-growth period has to be a direct function of how strong a company's competitive advantages are; the stronger these advantages, other things remaining equal, the longer a company can sustain high growth.

The discount rate when discounting cash flows to the company is always the cost of capital, which is the weighted average of cost of equity and cost of debt, using market value weights. Discounting the cash flows at the cost of capital provides the value of a company's operating assets. To this number, we add the value of cash and nonoperating assets and net out the value of the debt to get the value of the equity. Many companies have non-common-stock equity, such as warrants and management options. To come up with the value per share, we subtract non-common-stock equity from the value of the equity before dividing by the number of shares.

In the end, the value of a company can be written in terms of four inputs: the current free cash flows to the company, the length of the high-growth period, the growth rate during the period, and the cost of capital.

Estimation Issues

The real challenges in valuation are questions of estimation, not problems with the existing model. Investors need to revisit the fundamental aspects of the estimates required for DCF analysis. In the process, they may develop a better framework for looking at valuation.

Nominal versus Real Valuation. One of the first decisions in DCF analysis, especially for valuations of companies outside the United States, is the basic decision of whether to do valuations in nominal or in real terms. In theory, using nominal cash flows and nominal discount rates will produce the same value, but when inflation rises above 10 percent, DCF valuations start falling apart in nominal terms because they become extraordinarily sensitive to small changes in assumptions. The solution is to use real valuation or perform the valuation in a different currency.

In real valuations, we look at cash flows prior to considering inflation, and we discount them at real discount rates, which are also before inflation. Discounting real cash flows at the real discount rate yields the value of the company. The two biggest problems with this approach are that taxes are still computed based on nominal, not real, income and that estimating real risk-free rates and risk premiums is far more difficult.

An alternative is to do the valuation in a more stable currency. In Brazil, for example, DCF valuation is typically done in U.S. dollar terms. Analysts might think that using this approach means they do not have to worry about expected inflation in the Brazilian currency. Unfortunately, that is not true. For example, for Brahma, a major beverage company in Brazil, projecting the cash flows in dollars means first projecting in Brazilian reais and then converting the cash flows into dollars. Converting the cash flows into dollars requires expected exchange rates. Of course, simply using current exchange rates will not suffice. Because changes in exchange rates are driven by differences in inflation between the local currency and the U.S. dollar, doing this conversion requires analysts to project inflation rates.

The issue of consistency is not emphasized enough in valuation. We have to make sure that cash flows and discount rates are consistently estimated and that currency terms, whether nominal or real, are matched up correctly.

Cost of Equity. Consider the simplest approach of estimating cost of equity, which is a fundamental input in every valuation:

$$\text{Cost of equity} = R_f + \text{Equity beta} \times [E(R_m) - R_f],$$

where R_f is the risk-free rate and $E(R_m)$ is the expected return on the market index (diversified portfolio).

Estimating cost of equity requires three inputs: the risk-free rate, the risk premium, and beta. For the risk-free rate, the common practice is to use short-term government security rates. For setting a risk premium, the standard practice is to use a historical risk premium. For beta, the most common approach is to regress stock returns against market returns. Unfortunately, all three of these practices can provide misleading answers.

■ *Short-term government security rates.* For an investment to be risk free, the exact return over the life of the investment must be known. A six-month U.S. T-bill is not risk free for the purpose of considering an eight-year cash flow. It is not risk free because the investor has to reinvest it at the end of each six-month period—at a currently unknown rate. In this case, the appropriate risk-free rate is an eight-year zero-coupon government bond rate.

This requirement suggests that every single cash flow in a valuation will actually have a different risk-free rate, depending on when it comes due. As a practical matter, analysts could probably use some variant of duration matching. In the United States, the best solution is to use the long-term government bond as the risk-free rate.

U.S. investors assume that U.S. government securities are default free, and they use a government security rate as the risk-free rate. Outside the United States, however, this assumption is violated more often than not. The Brazilian government is not viewed as a default-free entity. So, one of the first problems is that the government itself might not be risk free. In such cases, coming up with the risk-free rate is a challenge. Thus, one of the challenges of applying valuation models outside the United States is coming up with risk-free rates in the first place.

■ *Historical premiums.* Many people who use the capital asset pricing model (CAPM) to come up with the cost of equity prefer to use historical premiums. They use historical data on stock and bond returns over a past period, determine the average return made on stocks and on a riskless asset over the period, and take the difference, which is the historical risk premium. Often, the number takes on a life of its own and we stop thinking about what the risk premium really means.

Whenever investors use the historical risk premium in valuation, they are implicitly assuming two things. The first assumption is that the risk aversion of investors has not changed in a systematic way over time. That is, the risk aversion of investors over a certain period (frequently, the period between 1926 and the present) is, on average, equal to the risk aversion of investors looking forward from this point in time. The second assumption is that the average-risk investment on which the premium is computed is, in fact, consistent over time.

What is also disturbing is that, although investors use the same historical data, they do not generally agree on a risk premium. Different investment banks and different valuation authorities use different numbers—5.0 percent, 5.5 percent, 6.0 percent. Risk premiums as high as 12.5 percent and as low as 3.0 percent have been in use at the same time.

How the historical risk premium is computed matters. The result depends on several factors: what historical period is used, what type of investment is defined as the risk-free rate, and whether the arithmetic average or the geometric average is used. For example, as shown in **Table 1**, if the arithmetic average premium for stocks over T-bills is used for the 1926–96 period, the risk premium is 8.76 percent, versus 5.91 percent for the geometric average over T-bonds.

Arguably, the best basis is to use geometric premiums over the T-bond rate, and the reason is simple. If the goal is long-term returns over, say, a 10-year horizon, the focus is the compounded return over the 10 years, not the arithmetic average return. The statistical rationale for using the arithmetic average premium does not hold up. In addition, if the choice for

Table 1. Various Historical Risk Premiums

Historical Period	Stocks minus T-Bills Arithmetic Mean	Stocks minus T-Bills Geometric Mean	Stocks minus T-Bonds Arithmetic Mean	Stocks minus T-Bonds Geometric Mean
1926–96	8.76%	6.95%	7.57%	5.91%
1962–96	5.74	4.63	5.16	4.46
1981–96	10.34	9.72	9.22	8.02

Note: See my World Wide Web site (www.stern.nyu.edu/~adamodar) for data on returns going back to 1926.

the risk-free rate is a T-bond rate, use a T-bond rate for the risk premium to be consistent. Mixing up the risk-free rate with a risk premium measured against a different definition of a risk-free rate is absurd.

Using as long a time period as possible is desirable, which is a little counterintuitive. After all, if the implied assumption is that risk aversion remains constant, does going back to 1926 make any sense? The reason for going back as far as possible is that each of the historical risk premiums in Table 1 comes with a standard error. For instance, the standard error for a 25-year estimate is roughly 5–6 percent. The easiest way to compute standard error is divide the standard deviation in equity on an annual basis by the square root of the number of years in the estimation. Effectively, this result means the range on your estimate is huge. So, the longer the historical time period, the lower the standard error.

This fact means that historical risk premiums for markets outside the United States are not reliable. These markets do not have the amount of historical data available in the United States. The ability to estimate a historical risk premium for Brazil or Indonesia means nothing because the standard error on any estimate will be far larger than the estimate itself. Even in markets that have 35–40 years of history, such as Germany, the standard error is often larger than the risk premium estimated on the basis of historical data.

A simple approach is helpful for estimating risk premiums in markets outside the United States. **Table 2** shows ratings for different Latin American countries. The ratings measure the default risk in the country bonds issued by these countries. The desired premium is an equity risk premium, so the task is to convert this bond rating into an equity risk premium. The conversion has two steps. First, estimate a default spread based on the rating. The spread can be estimated in one of two ways. One way is to use U.S. corporate bonds with the same rating (for Brazil, the equivalent is U.S. corporate bonds with a BB– rating) and determine the spread over U.S.-bonds. Another way is to look at the country–T-bond spread. In the

Table 2. Standard & Poor's Country Ratings for Latin America, June 1998

Country	Rating	Corporate Spread	Country Bond Spread
Argentina	BB	1.75%	2.58%
Brazil	BB–	2.00	2.87
Chile	A–	0.75	NA
Colombia	BBB–	1.50	NA
Paraguay	BB–	2.00	NA
Peru	BB	1.75	2.04
Uruguay	BBB–	1.50	1.68
Venezuela	B+	2.25	2.60

NA = not available.

Note: Ratings are foreign currency ratings. Country bond spreads based on par Brady bond, blended yield over T-bond.

---

case of Brazil, use the spread between a Brazilian government bond and the matching U.S. Treasury bond.

So, the first step provides a fixed-income spread. The task, however, is to estimate an equity risk premium. Bonds are less risky than equity, so if the fixed-income spread is 2 percent or 2.5 percent, the equity risk premium for Brazil has to be much larger. For example, to estimate the Brazilian equity risk premium, start with the 2 percent spread based on the rating and scale it by the relative volatility of the Brazilian equity market. For example, at one point, the volatility of the Bovespa, the Brazilian stock index, was about three times the volatility of the Brazilian C bond. Use this scaling factor to come up with a country risk premium for Brazil over and above a base equity premium.

In other words, for countries outside the United States, the risk premium has two components. First, a base equity premium is estimated by looking at a mature market, such as the United States. Second, a country risk premium is a function of the riskiness of this market. The riskier the country and the more volatile its equity market, the larger the country risk premium will be. In the case of Brazil, for example, take 5.5 percent as the base U.S. equity premium and add a 6.3 percent country risk premium to come up with a total equity risk premium of 11.8 percent. By allowing for the consideration of both country risk and the current volatility in the market, this method provides an estimate of the market's risk premium.

The final component, once the country risk premium has been established, is to come up with the cost of equity. There are three approaches for dealing with country risk premiums. To understand the potential differences between the three approaches, consider the following example in which all three approaches are applied to a Brazilian paper and pulp company called Aracruz Celulose. The analysis has been done completely in real terms, so this rate is the real risk-free rate, not one based on Brazilian currency. For the purposes of this illustration, the risk-free rate is 5 percent, the estimated beta is 0.72, the Brazilian country spread is 6.29 percent, and the base U.S. premium is 5.5 percent.

The first approach assumes that every company within a country is equally exposed to country risk, which means adding a constant to the cost of equity. In this approach, expected return is calculated as

$$E(\text{Return}) = \text{Risk-free rate} + \text{Country spread} + \text{Beta}(\text{U.S. risk premium}).$$

For example, in Brazil, this approach assumes that every Brazilian company is equally exposed to country risk.

Using this approach for Aracruz would work as follows:

$$E(\text{Return}) = 5\% + 6.29\% + 0.72(5.5\%) = 15.25\%.$$

Thus, under this approach, the Aracruz cost of equity is 15.25 percent.

The second approach assumes that exposure to country risk is proportional to exposure to all other market risk. Add the country spread into the base premium and multiply by the beta of the stock:

$$E(\text{Return}) = \text{Risk-free rate} + \text{Beta}(\text{U.S. premium} + \text{Country spread}).$$

In this approach, the example of Aracruz would take the following form:

$$E(\text{Return}) = 5\% + 0.72(5.5\% + 6.29\%) = 13.49\%.$$

Adding the 6.29 percent to the 5.5 percent produces a total country risk premium of 11.8 percent. Multiplying the country risk premium by the beta yields a cost of equity of 13.49 percent.

The third, and most flexible, way of approaching this issue is to assume that exposure to country risk can be different from exposure to all other risk. In this case, the cost of equity has three components: a risk-free rate, a beta times a mature market equity premium, and a lambda, which measures exposure to country risk times the country spread:

$$E(\text{Return}) = \text{Risk-free rate} + \text{Beta}(\text{U.S. premium}) + \lambda(\text{Country spread}).$$

This approach allows for looking at companies within a country and attaching a higher premium to companies that are overexposed to country risk or attaching a lower premium to companies that are underexposed to country risk. Once again, consider the case of Aracruz:

$$E(\text{Return}) = 5\% + 0.72(5.5\%) + 0.4(6.29\%) = 11.47\%.$$

In this case, lambda is determined in a simplistic manner by dividing the proportion of Aracruz's revenues that came in Brazilian reais by the proportion of a typical Brazilian company's revenues coming in Brazilian reais. Aracruz gets about 20 percent of its revenue in Brazilian currency because, as a paper and pulp company, it sells in a global market and gets most of its cash flows in dollars. The implicit assumption is that the lower the revenues from the local currency, the less the exposure to country risk. We divide the proportion of Aracruz's revenues that come in reais by the average Brazilian company's proportion of revenues in reais. This calculation produces a lambda for Aracruz of only 0.4, which means that Aracruz is less exposed to country risk than the typical Brazilian company because it gets so much of its cash flows in U.S. dollars. So, Aracruz's cost of equity under this approach is 11.47 percent.

This approach is the most flexible one and the one investors need to start using to estimate cost of equity. This framework is also effective for U.S. companies that get the bulk of their revenues overseas. If a U.S. company gets 75 percent of its revenues in Asia, using the U.S. market risk premium to evaluate it like any other U.S. company is a mistake. Investors have to start building into their discount rates some measure of country risk exposure. Doing so will affect valuations.

A different way of thinking about the risk premium (and, unfortunately, one that is not used enough in valuation) is to estimate an implied equity premium. In other words, let the market decide what the premium is.

Using a simple model, assume that investors have ready access to the following numbers—the current level of the S&P 500 Index, the expected dividends in stock buybacks next year for the entire index, and the expected growth rate in earnings and dividends over the next five years. If the growth rate is assumed to be stable, the value of stocks can be written as the basic Gordon growth model:

Value = Expected dividends and stock buybacks next year/(Required return on stocks − Expected growth rate)

For the value, plug in the current level of the index; for the expected dividends, plug in the expected dividends and stock buybacks on the S&P 500; for the expected growth rate, use an estimate from one of the forecast estimate providers, such as I/B/E/S International or Zacks. The only unknown input in this equation is the required return. Solve for the required return as if doing an internal rate of return for a capital budgeting problem. The required rate of return is the implied cost of equity—i.e., the implied rate of return that equity investors demand for investing in stocks.

As a quick estimate, for December 1998 data, the required return on the stocks was about 8.5 percent. In other words, in December 1998, stocks were being priced on the implicit rate of return of 8.5 percent. If stocks were being priced to earn 8.5 percent and the T-bond rate was 5.1 percent, the difference between these two numbers would be an implied equity premium of roughly 3.4 percent. The implied equity premium is a very different way of establishing risk premiums—different from looking at historical data.

For portfolio managers or equity analysts, using a historical premium of 5.5 percent or 6.0 percent or 7.4 percent when the implied equity premium in U.S. markets is closer to 3.0 percent will result in a lot of stocks looking overvalued. If the requirement is to do market-neutral valuation, which is often the case in portfolio management—not to pass judgment on the overall market but to find stocks that are under- or overvalued relative to the current market—the only way to do so in the context of DCF modeling is to switch from historical risk premiums to implied equity premiums.

Given this approach of estimating implied equity premiums, **Figure 1** shows the implied equity premium in the S&P 500 for every year from 1960 through 1996. The 1997 number is about 2.3 percent. The nice thing about implied equity premiums is that tracking them through time can reveal what fundamentals seem to cause implied equity premiums to rise. Between 1960 and 1970, for instance, the implied equity premium was between 3 and 4 percent. In the 1970s, it took off, peaking in 1978 at roughly 6.5 percent. So, when markets have come down, implied equity premiums have gone up—other things remaining equal. Since 1978, the implied equity premium has been on an overall downward trend.

At the end of 1997, the implied equity premium was the lowest it has been in 37 years, which can be read in one of two ways. One reading is to infer a paradigm shift—people are different, people are less risk averse, people have more pension money, people have longer time horizons, people are more globally diversified. Although each of these scenarios has an element of truth to it, another interpretation could be that implied equity premiums are low because prices are too high. The debate about implied equity premiums is really one about whether stocks are correctly valued (the implied equity premium is correct), undervalued (the premium is too high), or overvalued (the premium is too low).

One of the advantages of the implied equity premium is that it can be estimated for any market in the world. Historical data are not needed. Take the Argentine Merval stock index as an example. Use the level of the index as of June 1998 and the dividend yield on the index. Because of the lack of data on expected long-term growth in earnings for many Argentine stocks, use estimated growth rates on

Figure 1. Implied Equity Premium for S&P 500, 1960–96

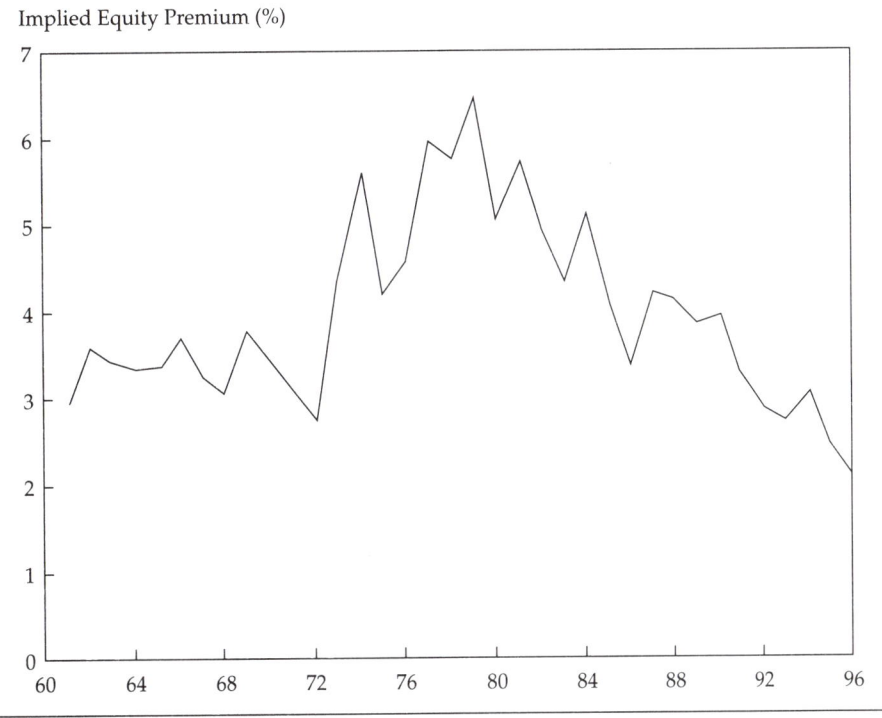

Argentine American Depositary Receipts as a proxy for the entire index; the estimated growth rate in earnings for the ADRs is 15 percent. Because the entire analysis is in U.S. dollar terms, use 6 percent as both the T-bond rate and as a measure of stable growth (after five years) as of June 1998. Using a two-stage dividend discount model with a 15 percent growth rate for the next five years and 6 percent thereafter provides a required rate of return for Argentine equities of 9.52 percent. Subtracting the 6 percent gives an implied equity premium of 3.5 percent. At that point in time, the U.S. equity premium was about 2.3 percent, so the Argentine premium was larger but not by the magnitude estimated using historical data.

Using the implied equity premium gives analysts a way to track equity premiums over time without relying on historical data. This method also allows analysts to estimate the implied equity premium for any market and do market-neutral valuations as of that point in time.

■ *Estimating beta.* The beta for an investment, at least on paper, comes from a simple regression. It is the slope coefficient from a regression of returns on the stock against returns on the market index:

$$R_j = a + bR_m,$$

where R_j represents stock returns and R_m is market returns.

Because empirical evidence suggests that, over time, betas tend to move toward 1, estimation services use some fixed weight—65/35, 60/40, 70/30, 67/33 (that is, for example, 0.65 times the raw beta plus 0.35 times 1)—to push betas toward 1.

The standard error of the beta is another significant issue. The median standard error for a beta estimate for a U.S. company is between 0.25 and 0.30. As the standard error increases, the range of uncertainty for the beta is so large that the beta estimate becomes useless.

Another phenomenon involving beta is common in most emerging markets, in which the top three or four companies may compose 60–70 percent of the index. For example, the Brazilian company Telebras (Telecomunicacoes Brasileiras) appears to have a very precise estimate of beta when regressed against the Bovespa stock index, with an R^2 of 70 percent and a standard deviation of 0.07. Telebras, however, accounts for 50 percent of the Bovespa, which is a trade-weighted index. Because Telebras is half of the trading volume in real terms at any point in time, the beta for Telebras would be little more than a regression of Telebras against itself.

Even for developed markets, this problem exists, although to a smaller degree. For example, in Germany, Allianz and DaimlerChrysler are each roughly 10 percent of the DAX, which is the local index used to estimate betas for German companies.

©2000, Association for Investment Management and Research

A key point is that beta measures the risk relative to a diversified portfolio. In order for Telebras to have a beta of 1.11 (which is the beta estimated against the Bovespa), the diversified portfolio to which the stock is added must consist of only Brazilian stocks held in proportion to their trading value. Because most services estimate betas for emerging market companies using the local index, these betas mean absolutely nothing if the stocks are for inclusion in a portfolio that includes nonlocal stocks. To be meaningful, the beta of every company ought to be estimated not against a local index but against a global index.

An even more troubling problem with beta is that the betas for emerging markets are completely counterintuitive. The largest and the safest companies look riskiest; the smallest and riskiest companies look safest. This phenomenon is caused by index domination. The weighted-average beta, for all stocks, is 1. Because Telebras has a beta greater than 1, all 177 other stocks in the index could conceivably have betas of less than 1 and still produce a weighted average of 1. The possibility is more than theoretical. Recently, only nine stocks in the Brazilian index had betas above 1, whereas 169 had betas below 1.

Three solutions to the regression beta problem exist. First, investors can modify the regression beta. One modification is to choose a different index. For example, one could estimate Telebras's beta by using its ADR and working with the S&P 500. A lot of U.S. investors use this approach, but it works only if a company has an ADR.

A second solution to the regression beta problem is to estimate the beta for a company without using the regression. A measure called the "relative standard deviation" is a useful proxy for relative risk and does not require running a regression of stock prices against the index. Instead of a regression, this method uses the standard deviation of stock prices. Dividing each company's individual standard deviation by the market average produces a number for relative volatility that looks very much like a beta. It will be scaled around 1; a number above 1 is above-average risk and below 1 is below-average risk. Not only does this relative volatility look like beta but it can be used exactly like beta. Wherever beta is used in the CAPM, plug in the relative volatility. The implicit assumption is that total risk and market risk are perfectly correlated, but given how much trouble arises in estimating market risk, relative volatility is a useful approximation for the risk of a company.

A third solution is to estimate the beta from the bottom up. Bottom-up beta arguably provides a far better estimate of a company's beta than top-down beta, which is what regression beta is. Knowing what a company's business is permits the estimation of its beta without ever running a company-specific regression. Begin by getting the unlevered betas for the company's core businesses by looking up the unlevered betas for other companies in those businesses, taking out the financial leverage because the company might have no debt or might have a lot of debt. Take a weighted average of these unlevered betas (weighted by the proportion of operating income that comes from each type of business). Next, lever up using the company's debt-to-equity ratio.

This approach offers greater precision by substituting the average beta of the sector in which the company operates for the regression beta. The advantage of using an average is that the average of a lot of noisy betas still can be fairly precise. Noise averages out, and the result is an estimated beta that is precise even though the industry's individual betas are noisy. In addition, this approach also reflects the current leverage of the company.

Consider Walt Disney Company in 1997. Using return data from five years produces a beta of 1.35. Two years into this regression, Disney bought Capital Cities/ABC for $18.5 billion. In the process, Disney borrowed $12 billion, and the regression does not fully reflect this leverage. This inability to capture current leverage is part of the reason bottom-up betas make a lot more sense. **Table 3** shows an estimate of Disney's bottom-up beta. Disney is in five businesses: Creative Content is movies; Retailing is the Disney stores; Broadcasting is Cap Cities and the Disney cable channel; Theme Parks are obvious; and Real Estate is Disney real estate ventures.

Using the comparable companies, we get an unlevered beta for each sector. We use Disney debt-to-equity ratio for the first four divisions because these divisions do not borrow on their own and Disney borrows for them. The Real Estate division is the only one that has its own debt-to-equity ratio. With a beta for each division and a cost of equity for each, the weighted average of those betas, weighted by the operating income from each, is a bottom-up beta for Disney of 1.09 in unlevered terms and 1.25 in levered terms. The advantage of this approach is that it is generic and can be applied to private companies, small companies, large companies, and even initial public offerings.

Value Creation

With a traditional discounted cash flow model, the value of a company can be enhanced in four basic ways. First, companies can increase cash flows from existing assets, either by increasing after-tax earnings from assets in place or by reducing the reinvestment necessary to maintain these assets.

Table 3. Estimated Walt Disney Company Bottom-Up Betas, 1997

Business	Unlevered Beta	Debt-to-Equity Ratio	Levered Beta	Risk-Free Rate	Risk Premium	Cost of Equity
Disney	1.09	21.97%	1.25	7.00%	5.50%	13.85%
Creative Content	1.25	20.92	1.42	7.00	5.50	14.80
Retailing	1.50	20.92	1.70	7.00	5.50	16.35
Broadcasting	0.90	20.92	1.02	7.00	5.50	12.61
Theme Parks	1.10	20.92	1.26	7.00	5.50	13.91
Real Estate	0.70	59.27	0.92	7.00	5.50	12.31

Second, companies can increase the expected growth rate, either by increasing the reinvestment rate or, better still, increasing the return on the reinvestments.

The third way to enhance value is to extend the high-growth period. In DCF analysis, excess return (i.e., earning more than the cost of capital) drives growth. For this effect to be true, the company must have some barrier to entry, because in a competitive marketplace, excess return acts as a magnet. So, lengthening the high-growth period requires figuring out a way to increase the barriers to entry.

Fourth, reducing the cost of capital will enhance value. Companies can diminish cost of capital by reducing the operating risk in investments and assets, changing the financial mix, or changing the financing composition.

Ultimately, these four actions are the only ways to create value. The converse of this proposition is that, by definition, an action that does not affect cash flows, the growth rate, the length of the growth period, or the cost of capital cannot affect value.

Value-Neutral Actions. Arguably, 80 percent of what companies do is value neutral. Such activity may generate publicity, but it has no effect on value. For example, a number of accounting decisions affect reported earnings but not cash flows, including
- changing inventory methods from FIFO to LIFO or vice versa in financial reports but not for tax purposes,
- changing the depreciation method used in financial reports (but not the tax books) from accelerated to straight-line depreciation, and
- taking major noncash restructuring charges that reduce reported earnings but are not tax deductible.

These actions are value neutral because they do not affect cash flows, the growth rate, the length of the growth period, or the cost of capital.

A good example of value-neutral activity is what happens in acquisitions. Many acquisitions are rejected because the acquiring company cannot use a pooling accounting treatment to do the acquisition. The distinction between purchase accounting and pooling accounting is that in pooling, the book values are added up—with no amortization of goodwill and thus no effect on earnings. In purchase accounting, the difference between the price paid and the book value shows up as goodwill, which then is amortized over time.

Amortization of goodwill does not affect cash flows because it is not a tax-deductible expense and thus does not affect taxes. It also does not affect the expected growth rate because marginal investments stay the same whether purchase or pooling is used. Amortization of goodwill does not affect the length of the high-growth period because it cannot increase the barriers to entry for competition. Finally, it does affect cost of capital. Although the decision to use purchase or pooling is value neutral, companies spend great amounts of time, energy, and resources trying to get a pooling treatment rather than a purchase treatment for their acquisitions.

Value-Enhancing Actions. Companies can create value in only a limited number of ways. Understanding the true paths to value creation is vital to investors' ability to cut through financial noise and focus on the critical areas of performance.

Exhibit 1 shows the value enhancement chain. On one dimension are the four categories that value enhancement affects—cash flows from assets in place, the expected growth rate, the length of the high-growth period, and the cost of financing. The other dimension consists of possible ways to create value within the four categories. The first column represents actions that are immediate value creators, with no trade-off involved. The second column captures actions that involve some kind of trade-off but that probably will work to increase value. The third column is actions that "could work if" competitors cooperate.

The following discussion evaluates the possible actions within each category of value enhancement:

Assets in place. For cash flows from assets in place, value-enhancing actions that produce immediate results are divestiture and cost cutting. Divestiture and cost cutting, however, can backfire. For example, a divestiture strategy's results may be immediate, but the right targets for elimination or reduction are not always obvious. A common mis-

Exhibit 1. The Value Enhancement Chain

Area of Value Enhancement	Has an Immediate Effect	Probably Will Work	Could Work If...
Cash flows from assets in place	Divest assets/projects with divestiture value greater than continuing value	Reduce net working-capital requirements by reducing inventory and accounts receivable or by increasing accounts payable	Change pricing strategy to maximize the product of profit margins and turnover ratio
	Terminate projects with liquidation value greater than continuing value	Reduce capital maintenance expenditures on assets in place	
	Eliminate operating expenses that generate no current revenues and no growth		
Expected growth rate	Eliminate new capital expenditures that are expected to earn less than the cost of capital	Increase reinvestment rate or marginal return on capital or both in company's existing businesses	Increase reinvestment rate or marginal return on capital or both in new businesses
Length of high-growth period	If any of the company's products or services can be patented and protected, do so	Use economies of scale or cost advantages to create higher return on capital	Build up brand name
			Increase the cost of switching from product and reduce cost of switching to it
Cost of financing	Use swaps and derivatives to match debt more closely to company's assets	Change financing type and use innovative securities to reflect the types of assets being financed	Reduce the operating risk of the company by making products less discretionary to customers
	Recapitalize to move the company toward its optimal debt ratio	Use the optimal financing mix to finance new investments	
		Make cost structure more flexible to reduce operating leverage	

take is to think that a value-enhancing strategy is simply to get rid of poor projects or divisions that are not earning their required rate of return. This view is mistaken because what matters is not how much is invested in the divisions but how much they are worth if divested.

If the divestiture value of the division is greater than the value of the division continuing in the company, divestiture makes sense. The challenge is to divest or liquidate only those projects for which the divestiture or liquidation value actually exceeds the continuing value and to eliminate only those operating expenses that truly do not create revenues.

In terms of actions that probably will get results, companies can increase the cash flows from assets in place by reducing the net working-capital requirements. This change does affect cash flows. Reducing inventories to 3 percent of revenues from 7 percent of revenues will make a large impact on value.

Another action that will probably enhance value is reducing capital maintenance expenditures. Think of capital expenditures coming from two sources—maintaining existing assets and creating future growth. Reducing capital maintenance expenditures on assets in place will increase the cash flows from assets in place and thus increase value.

■ *Expected growth.* The immediate action for improving expected growth is to eliminate new capital expenditures for which the return on capital is less than the cost of capital. Such expenditures are obviously value destroying.

An action that probably will work is increasing the reinvestment rate or the marginal return on capital—or preferably both—for the company's *existing* businesses, thereby increasing the growth rate.

An action with much less certainty of success is to increase the reinvestment rate and/or increase the marginal return on capital for the company's *new* businesses.

■ *Length of high-growth period.* Actions for lengthening the high-growth period all boil down to increasing barriers to entry. The only immediate action in this area is to make sure that all eligible products are patented and protected. Actions that probably will work are improving economies of scale and enhancing cost advantages.

The most uncertain actions involve building up brand names or increasing the cost of switching away from the product and reducing the cost of switching to it. Brand advantages are a tremendous barrier to entry in some markets and allow companies to maintain high returns on capital and high value. In high-tech industries, the biggest barrier to entry is the cost of switching. For example, in the software industry, a company might come up with a better spreadsheet program than Microsoft Excel, but getting existing customers to switch to the new program would be tough because the cost of switching is so large, especially for large businesses.

■ *Cost of financing.* Immediate enhancement of value through cost of financing is possible in two ways. First, the cash flows on financing should have the same characteristics as the cash flows of the assets being financed. In other words, long-term assets should get long-term financing, dollar assets should have dollar financing; and so forth. Making the financing reflect the asset structure reduces the company's risk; reducing the company's risk reduces its cost of capital; and reducing its cost of capital increases its value.

The second immediate action that will increase value is moving toward the optimal debt ratio.

Three actions probably will work to enhance value through cost of financing. The first approach is to change the financing type and use innovative securities to reflect the types of assets being financed, and the second approach is to use the optimal financing mix to finance new investments.

The third action that is likely to work is to make the cost structure more flexible. Over the past 5–10 years, U.S. companies talked about flexibility but, in fact, they were simply trying to make their cost structure a function of their revenue levels. So, if a company can make wages much more of a function of how well the company is doing (e.g., in negotiation with the unions), it can increase the proportion of its costs that are variable. One of the payoffs to this approach is that the company's beta goes down: The lower the proportion of costs that are fixed costs, the lower the beta will be. Having a lot of fixed costs exaggerates risk. Having a lot of variable costs reduces risk by making the cost structure more flexible—reduce the risk, reduce the cost of capital.

A long-term, "could work if . . ." way of reducing the cost of financing is to try to reduce the operating risk of the company.

Effectively, the approaches described in this section summarize all the different ways of thinking about enhancing value. Actions that enhance value must affect one of four areas: cash flows from assets in place, expected growth, length of growth period, or cost of capital. Enhancing value through any other means is impossible. The other important consideration is the probability of a particular action succeeding. Even in a traditional valuation model, showing the effect of value-enhancing actions is straightforward.

Alternative Approaches to Enhancing Value. Alternative ways of enhancing value, which claim the advantage of simplicity, do exist. The alternative methods seek to maximize a variable that is correlated with the company's value. Possible targets are (and historically have been) accounting variables, such as earnings or return on investment; marketing variables, such as market share; and surplus value measures, such as EVA.

The danger of focusing on these variables is that the underlying assumption that these variables are correlated with value might be wrong. In the 1970s and 1980s, Japanese companies concentrated on increasing market share. They assumed that increasing their market share increased their value, but many of these companies subsequently learned that this assumption is not necessarily true. The advantage of such alternative approaches is that they have fewer variables than DCF valuation. The disadvantage is that this simplicity comes with a cost.

Economic Value Added

Economic value added is a measure of surplus value created by an investment. This approach defines the return on capital as the "true" cash flow return on capital earned on an investment. It also defines the cost of capital as the weighted average of the costs of the different financing instruments used to finance the investment. EVA has three basic inputs—invested capital, return on capital, and cost of capital:

$$EVA = (\text{Return on capital} - \text{Cost of capital}) \times (\text{Capital invested in project})$$

"Capital invested in project" is designed to capture how much capital is invested in assets in place, projects that are already active. How is invested capital measured? Some people might think market value is a potential measure. One of the problems of market value of companies is that market value includes expected future growth (in addition to assets in place). So, market value is out of the question as a potential measure. The next choice is book value. Is the accounting measure of book value really a measure of the market value of assets in place? Not always and not generally. To get from book value to capital investments, four adjustments are typically used: One adjustment is operating leases. For example, the balance sheet of The Gap has only equity—no debt.

The problem is that The Gap leases all of its stores and qualifies the leases as operating leases. In accounting terms, operating leases are operating expenses and do not show up on the balance sheet. The Gap has operating leases of half a billion dollars a year, the equivalent of almost $4–$5 billion in debt. So, to get The Gap's total invested capital, use the book equity plus the present value of operating leases. This approach is a more accurate measure of invested capital than simply taking the book value of capital found in the balance sheet.

The second adjustment for invested capital involves research and development expenses. Computing the EVA for high-tech companies, such as Intel Corporation or Microsoft, will produce an absurdly small book value of capital. The reason is simple: The accounting convention, at least in the United States, is that R&D expenses must be expensed and cannot be capitalized. As a consequence, although a company may have $2–$3 billion in R&D expenses and may be creating very valuable assets from these expenses, the R&D expenses never show up on the balance sheet. So, the adjustment is to capitalize R&D expenses. Simply add up the R&D expenses over time and treat them like any other asset.

The third adjustment is for one-time charges that reduce invested capital. Goodwill amortization is a classic example of such a one-time charge. Writing off goodwill reduces the invested capital. In computing the capital invested in assets in place, add back all of the variables that make invested capital look smaller than is the case.

The fourth type of adjustment, which tends to be small, involves accounting adjustments. The task is to account for the kind of game playing—switching from FIFO to LIFO or LIFO to FIFO, and so forth—that occurs at the margin to change operating earnings, which affects capital.

External analysts' EVA estimates will always be inferior to the EVA estimate made by someone working for the company. For example, a few years ago, one publishing company came up with a huge return on invested capital for their publishing division, something like 1,787 percent. The reason for the high number was that the assets of the publishing division were all copyrights and trademarks, which effectively had been amortized almost down to zero. So, when computing return on capital, the company was dividing the operating income by an unusually small number.

Of course, equity research analysts or portfolio managers working outside the company would not have a listing of every copyright and trademark the company owns and thus would be limited in what they could evaluate. Instead, they must work with book capital and make rough adjustments. The older the company, the less accuracy book capital can have as a measure of invested capital.

The other two components of EVA, "return on capital" and "cost of capital," also have limitations. The return on capital that analysts would like to measure is the return on investments already in place. The cost of capital should be a market value of cost of capital. Some people compute EVA using book value weights for debt and equity, to maintain consistency with the use of book value in measuring capital invested. This practice is not appropriate, and the cost of capital used in EVA calculations has to be exactly the same cost of capital as is used for DCF valuation, which is a market-value-weighted cost of capital. Using book cost of capital will systematically overstate the EVA of every company in the United States.

EVA Caveats. When companies adopt EVA, they are judging their managers based on this year's EVA versus an expected number. In other words, as long as managers deliver an EVA next year that is higher than some benchmark, they will be rewarded, usually with no upper limit on compensation.

A company can deliver a higher EVA than expected—while making stockholders worse off—in three ways. The first option is the "capital invested game." Bringing down the company's invested capital will make EVA look much better, even if the effect is purely cosmetic—especially if it is purely cosmetic. Increasing stock buybacks or taking large restructuring charges will generally lower capital and increase EVA.

The second possibility is the "growth game." In other words, the company tries to make next year's EVA look better by stealing from future growth. Thus, cutting back on R&D or expenses designed to generate future growth may improve EVA in the short term while reducing value in the long term. The CEO may end up with a bonus, but the stockholders get lower value.

The third option is "the risk game." The value of the company is the present value of EVA. So, if the company delivers a higher EVA but at a much higher cost of capital because the company has become riskier, stockholders are worse off because the company has exposed them to more risk.

Investors also face caveats for EVA. Portfolio managers who invest in the companies with the highest EVA or the highest increase in EVA, in the hope of earning excess returns, will fail. The reason is that market prices are driven not by the magnitude of the actual EVA but by the actual EVA versus expectations. The companies with the highest EVA may not necessarily make a great portfolio. More desirable are the companies for which the EVAs will be much higher than expected—because expectation is what determines stock prices.

Richard Bernstein, with Merrill Lynch & Company, did two studies (Bernstein 1997 and Bernstein 1998) on the effectiveness of using EVA for investing. First, he looked at 12-month returns by buying the top 10 percent of companies in terms of EVA. This portfolio returned about 1 percent less than the S&P 500 during the period studied. Next, he looked at companies that had the highest increase in EVA over the previous year. A portfolio of 50 companies drawn from the 10 percent of companies with the highest increase in EVA over the previous year would have done even worse.

Comparing EVA and DCF Valuation. In addition to value enhancement, EVA can also be used as a traditional valuation tool. In fact, analysts can write the value of a company as a sum of three components—the investment in existing assets plus the net present value (NPV) of the existing assets in place plus the NPV of all future projects. In terms of EVA, the value of a company can be written as the capital invested in assets in place plus the present value of EVA from assets in place plus the present value of EVA from all future projects.

To understand the relationship between EVA and DCF, consider the following comparison of EVA valuation of a company with the DCF valuation of the same company. The company for this example has assets in place worth $100 million. In other words, it has invested $100 million in assets in place. The after-tax operating income on assets in place is $15 million. This return on capital of 15 percent is expected to continue in the future, and the company's cost of capital is 10 percent. At the beginning of each of the next five years, the company is expected to make investments of $10 million each. These investments are also expected to earn 15 percent as a return on capital, and the cost of capital is expected to remain 10 percent. After Year 5, the company will continue to make investments and earnings will grow 5 percent a year, but the new investments will have a return on capital of only 10 percent, which is also the cost of capital. All assets and investments are expected to have infinite lives.

■ *EVA valuation*. The company's EVA from assets in place is $5 million (15 percent – 10 percent × $100 million). At the beginning of each of the next five years, the company will invest an additional $10 million in new investments, which will also earn a 5 percent spread, bringing in positive EVA. For simplicity, in the NPV calculation, assume that all investments have infinite lives. After Year 5, this company will keep growing, but the investments it takes on after Year 5 will earn exactly the cost of capital. So, the company's EVA valuation is $170.85 million, as follows:

Capital invested in assets in place	$100.00
+ Present value of EVA from assets in place = (0.15 – 0.10)(100)/0.10	50.00
+ Present value of EVA from new investments in Year 1 = (0.15 – 0.10)(10)/0.10	5.00
+ . . . Year 2 = [(0.15 –0.10)(10)/0.10]/1.1	4.55
+ . . . Year 3 = [(0.15 –0.10)(10)/0.10]/1.1^2	4.13
+ . . . Year 4 = [(0.15 –0.10)(10)/0.10]/1.1^3	3.76
+ . . . Year 5 = [(0.15 –0.10)(10)/0.10]/1.1^4	3.42
Value of company	$170.85

One insight that comes from this approach is that what creates value is not simply growth but growth with excess returns.

■ *DCF valuation*. Traditional DCF valuation is after-tax operating income minus net capital expenditures, discounted back at the cost of capital. The value of the company from a traditional DCF valuation is $170.85 million, as shown in **Table 4**.

Obviously, the value from DCF valuation is exactly the same value that is derived by taking the present value of EVA over time. If the same assumptions are used, the same answer should result with both DCF and EVA. The policy of maximizing the present value of your EVA over time is exactly equivalent to a policy of maximizing DCF value.

Conclusion

There are no shortcuts in valuation. The value of a company is a function of the company's cash flows, its expected growth, the length of the growth period and the cost of capital. To enhance value, therefore, we have to change one or more of these variables. Any approach that claims that it has found a simpler path to value creation is misleading.

Much of what we see as new and different in value enhancement is neither new nor different. The methods all have their roots in traditional discounted cash flow valuation.

Table 4. A Discounted Cash Flow Valuation
(in dollar millions)

Input	0	1	2	3	4	5	Terminal Year
EBIT $(1-t)$ from assets in place	$0.00	$15.00	$15.00	$15.00	$15.00	$15.00	
EBIT $(1-t)$ from investments, Year 1		1.50	1.50	1.50	1.50	1.50	
EBIT $(1-t)$ from investments, Year 2			1.50	1.50	1.50	1.50	
EBIT $(1-t)$ from investments, Year 3				1.50	1.50	1.50	
EBIT $(1-t)$ from investments, Year 4					1.50	1.50	
EBIT $(1-t)$ from investments, Year 5						1.50	
Total EBIT $(1-t)$		16.50	18.00	19.50	21.00	22.50	$23.63
Net capital expenditures	10.00	10.00	10.00	10.00	10.00	11.25	11.81
Future cash flows		6.50	8.00	9.50	11.00	11.25	11.81
Present value of future cash flows		5.91	6.61	7.14	7.51	6.99	
Terminal value						236.25	
Present value of terminal value	($10.00)					146.69	
Value of company	$170.85						
Return on capital	15%	15%	15%	15%	15%	15%	10%
Cost of capital	10%	10%	10%	10%	10%	10%	10%

Note: EBIT = Earnings before interest and taxes.

Question and Answer Session
Aswath Damodaran

Question: What is your preferred method of finding the risk premium?

Damodaran: Using an implied equity premium is the most useful approach, especially in emerging markets. In the United States, if conservative estimates are available, historical premiums can be useful, but implied premiums are still preferable. Even then, if you want to use mean reversion or if you do not like the fact that today's implied equity premium is low, you can use an implied equity premium averaged over time.

Question: If a high-P/E company acquires a low-P/E company and thus has instant earnings, how do you view the cost of capital for the acquisition?

Damodaran: If a high-P/E company acquires a low-P/E company, use the same test as for value. The acquisition does not increase cash flows collectively for the company. It does not increase the growth rate on a weighted-average basis. It has no effect on the length of the growth period. As for cost of capital, if a composite cost of capital is used, it will be a weighted average. Companies can create value only by taking actions that affect one of those four components. Essentially, the net present value of the acquisition is what drives value.

Question: With so many companies adopting EVA, are they learning that leveraging the balance sheet to buy back stock is a way to achieve the EVA?

Damodaran: These companies are learning that the easiest way to increase EVA is to bring down invested capital. Companies tried initially to increase earnings, which takes too much work. Instead, they found a much easier way to increase EVA. Companies that have adopted EVA have exhibited a progressive depletion in book capital, whether through stock buybacks or through something else. These companies know they look a lot better if they have less invested capital at play.

Financial Reporting and Disclosure for Equity Analysis

Paul R. Brown
Chair, Department of Accounting, Taxation, and Business Law
New York University Stern School of Business

> In the complex circumstances of the current reporting environment, financial statement analysis often presents challenges that cannot be addressed with a direct, quantitative approach. Analysts can benefit by beginning the evaluation process with information other than the raw numbers and focusing particular attention on understanding the economic characteristics of a company's industry, identifying company strategies, and "cleansing" the financial statement. The perspective gained from these efforts can help analysts interpret peculiar aspects of financial statement analysis, such as accounting for such "soft" assets as research and development.

The current investing and lending environment is constantly changing, and as a result, financial statement analysis has become more challenging than in the past. Analysts often contend with difficult questions: How can they value a company that reports losses or, in some cases, barely any revenue? What type of information is most helpful for evaluating companies that are primarily driven by highly complex demands of human capital and technology? To further complicate matters, analysts must fit this new information into a reporting model that has not changed for roughly 100 years (despite unmerciful tinkering by the Financial Accounting Standards Board [FASB] and the U.S. Securities and Exchange Commission [SEC]).

This presentation discusses a model of financial statement analysis that may be helpful in this complex environment and provides some illustrations of the model, particularly emphasizing nonrecurring items along with intangibles and other "soft assets." The presentation concludes by examining disclosure issues for an important soft asset—research and development.

Analysis Model

Financial statement analysis is hard work. Nothing can substitute for a high degree of dedication and perseverance or for a well-thought-out plan for approaching the task at hand. An effective financial statement analysis model consists of the following five steps:

- Identify economic characteristics.
- Identify company strategies.
- Understand and "cleanse" the financial statements.
- Analyze profitability and risk.
- Value the firm.

This five-step interrelated sequence is rather straightforward, but it demands an uncompromising attention to detail and due diligence. This presentation focuses on the first three steps, which is not to say that steps four and five are unimportant. Although analyzing profitability and risk and valuing the firm are vital steps, any analyst who attempts to reach conclusions in these areas without spending time on the first three steps is at a real loss. The first three steps are especially significant for industries that have assets that are not captured on the balance sheet, such as human capital and technology.

For such industries, analysts have to decide how to capture these assets (by pursuing steps one through three) or simply abandon the traditional reporting system altogether. For example, America Online's current subscriber base of more than 14 million is probably its most important asset. Can analysts value this asset on an ongoing basis or only in an auction? Some rather strange yardsticks, such as capitalized revenue stream per subscriber, exist for valuing these atypical assets. The solution is not for analysts to throw out the numbers for situations in which the numbers are simply not helpful. Rather, for some situations, analysts have to start with something other than the numbers, hence the need for steps one through three. Because corporate America is constantly changing, none of the three steps is easy to carry out. Even something as basic as determining exactly what a company does is not always easy, and at times, an analyst may not even be sure what industry a company belongs to. The first three steps, therefore, are crucial and not to be treated lightly.

Identifying Economic Characteristics and Company Strategies

To successfully navigate the first two steps, the analyst must know the industry thoroughly, understand the strategies used by the companies being analyzed, and in particular, recognize the information content of past financial *and* nonfinancial statements made by the company's management. This section illustrates the particular importance of identifying relevant economic characteristics and company strategies.

Identifying Economic Characteristics. Effective analysis first requires identifying the economic characteristics of the company's particular industry. The economic characteristics of an industry play a key role in dictating the types of financial relationships the analyst might observe in financial statements or summary statistics (i.e., ratios). So, the first step in the analytical model can be characterized as the macro-level analysis that goes into analyzing any company.

The economic characteristics of an industry, particularly as revealed in the financial statements, evoke such questions as the following: Does technological change play an important role in the company's ability to maintain a competitive advantage, as in the software industry? Does the industry include a small number of competitors who sell specialized products, as in the pharmaceutical industry? Does the industry have high barriers to entry, as in the telecommunications industry? These types of questions begin the analysis, followed by company-specific issues of strategy.

Identifying Company Strategies. To understand a company's strategy, the analyst must scrutinize both what the company says about its strategic plans and the actions the company takes to implement a plan. Some analysts say that they rely totally on the corporate disclosures and reports and that they do not spend time with management at all. Such analysts are constantly comparing past statements with actions—to see what was stated and then see what happens, say, three quarters later. Analysts should also notice what management does not say and compare what is left unsaid with what was said six months or a year earlier.

Illustrations. The issues important to understanding an industry are countless, but a few examples can at least illustrate the numbers side of industry analysis. The key to understanding an industry and a company is at the product level. **Figure 1** shows the typical revenue, net income, and cash flow for a product at various stages of the product's life cycle. Individual products move during their lives through four stages: introduction, growth, maturity, and decline. Panel A shows the typical revenue cycle for the four stages; Panel B shows how net income turns from negative to positive to negative again; Panel C shows the cash flow patterns. At the early growth stages for products, companies probably are reporting barely any profit (or revenue). In addition, when most prod-

Figure 1. Typical Revenue, Net Income, and Cash Flow Patterns at Various Stages of a Product's Life Cycle

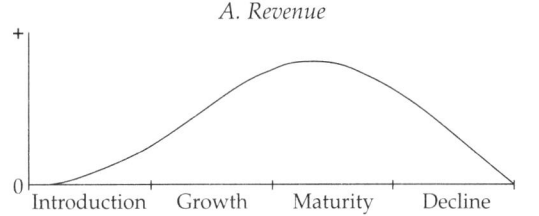

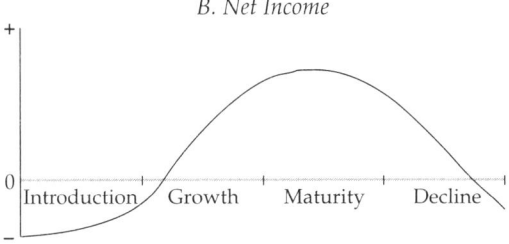

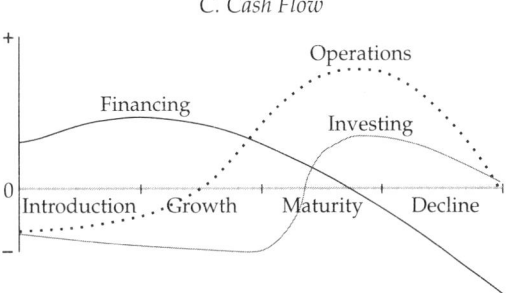

Source: Based on data from Clyde P. Stickney and Paul R. Brown, *Financial Reporting and Statement Analysis: A Strategic Perspective* (Fort Worth, TX:Dryden/Harcourt Brace College Publishers, 1999).

ucts are at their introduction and growth stages, the companies are always generating negative cash flows from operations. They need cash, which they get from external sources—either ownership equity or credit equity. They also need that cash to cover their negative investing cash flows. That is, they are using the financing funds to invest. The business is not generating cash at this point, as shown by the cash flows from operations in Panel C. These cash flow patterns for the industry and company under scrutiny exemplify an important industry characteristic and company demographic that the analyst would want to understand. For example, analysts typically say that if a business does not generate positive operating cash flows from its operations for a certain number of years, that business will probably fail.

Figure 1 represents information for a one-product company. Clearly, this analysis becomes more complicated for multiproduct companies. It requires a weighting of the various products and a conclusion about the average life cycle of the products. By analogy, Figure 1 can be thought of as representing a one-company industry, and multicompany industries would be handled similarly to multiproduct companies.

Netscape Communications Corporation's income and cash flows illustrate this cycle, as shown in **Table 1**. Netscape's first major year of operation was 1994, which represented a rapid growth phase of Netscape's life cycle. The company operated at a loss in 1994 (net income of nearly –$14 million) but subsequently improved during the next two years, with a smaller loss in 1995 than in 1994 and positive profits in 1996. Cash flow from operations was also negative in 1994 but turned positive (roughly $12 million) in 1995 and continued to increase in 1996.

Both cash flow and earnings were negative in 1994, but cash flow was less markedly so; although both subsequently improved, cash flow improved more rapidly than earnings. Why? The line item that matters most is "increase (decrease) in other current liabilities," which for 1996 was $74 million. Those are deferred revenues, created because Netscape received substantial cash from its customers before it provided services. This cash would not be reported as revenue, but it did improve Netscape's cash flow from operations. The point is that during the period, there was a reason why cash flow from operations was at first much less negative and later much more positive than net income—a lot of up-front cash being received from

Table 1. Netscape Communications Corporation Statement of Cash Flows
(US$ in thousands)

Line Item	1994	1995	1996
Operations			
Net income	($13,830)	($6,613)	$20,908
Depreciation	345	3,853	16,320
Other addbacks	0	2,553	2,456
Other subtractions	0	0	23,747
Working capital provided by operations	($13,485)	($207)	$15,937
Increase (decrease) in receivables	(1,688)	(24,929)	(83,525)
Increase (decrease) in other current assets	(298)	(5,989)	(10,473)
Increase (decrease) in accounts payable	1,506	6,696	18,951
Increase (decrease) in other current liabilities	6,845	36,437	74,197
Cash flow from operations	($7,120)	$12,008	$15,087
Investing			
Fixed assets acquired	($3,175)	($20,522)	($81,931)
Change in marketable securities	—	(116,367)	(87,120)
Other investing transactions	(1,089)	(2,891)	(5,363)
Cash flow from investing	($14,264)	($139,780)	$174,414
Financing			
Increase in long-term borrowing	0	$2,200	0
Issue of capital stock	$17,852	171,059	$192,182
Decrease in long-term borrowing	–504	–401	–601
Cash flow from financing	$17,348	$172,858	$191,581
Change in cash	$5,964	$45,086	$32,254
Cash—beginning of year	4,226	10,190	55,276
Cash—end of year	$10,190	$55,276	$87,530
Growth in revenues from previous year	—	1,963.5%	305.4%

customers. The more important point is that analysts who ignore industry economics and how they translate to particular company strategies do so at their own peril.

Figure 2 is another attempt to use numbers—in this case, ROA (return on assets), profit margin, and asset turnover—to say something about an industry and its characteristics. Specifically, Figure 2 shows, for a 10-year period (1987–1996), the median annual ROA, profit margin, and asset turnover data for 22 industries. The isoquants reflect ROA at 3 percent and 6 percent. For any point on the isoquant labeled 6 percent, a combination of profit margin and asset turnover produces an ROA of 6 percent; the 3 percent isoquant is similarly interpreted. For example, an ROA of 6 percent can result from a 6 percent profit margin with only a one-time turnover of assets. At the other extreme, the 6 percent ROA can come from a 1 percent profit margin with a six times average turnover. The companies in the grocery store industry, for instance, turned over their assets three times but only earned a 2 percent profit margin on their products, thus giving the grocery industry an ROA of 6 percent.

Analysts can also delve within an industry to perform the same kind of analysis for sectors of the industry. **Table 2** shows such an approach for three sectors within each of three industries—forest products, apparel, and food. What is noteworthy in Table 2 is the extent to which an aggregate industry analysis may mask important differences within the industry. Within the forest products industry, for instance, substantial turnover differences exist between the paper processing and the printing and publishing sectors.

Table 2 implies an important lesson: Analysts should never be content with only the kind of aggregate or even subaggregate analysis contemplated in

Figure 2. Average Median ROA, Profit Margin, and Asset Turnover for 22 Industries, 1987–96

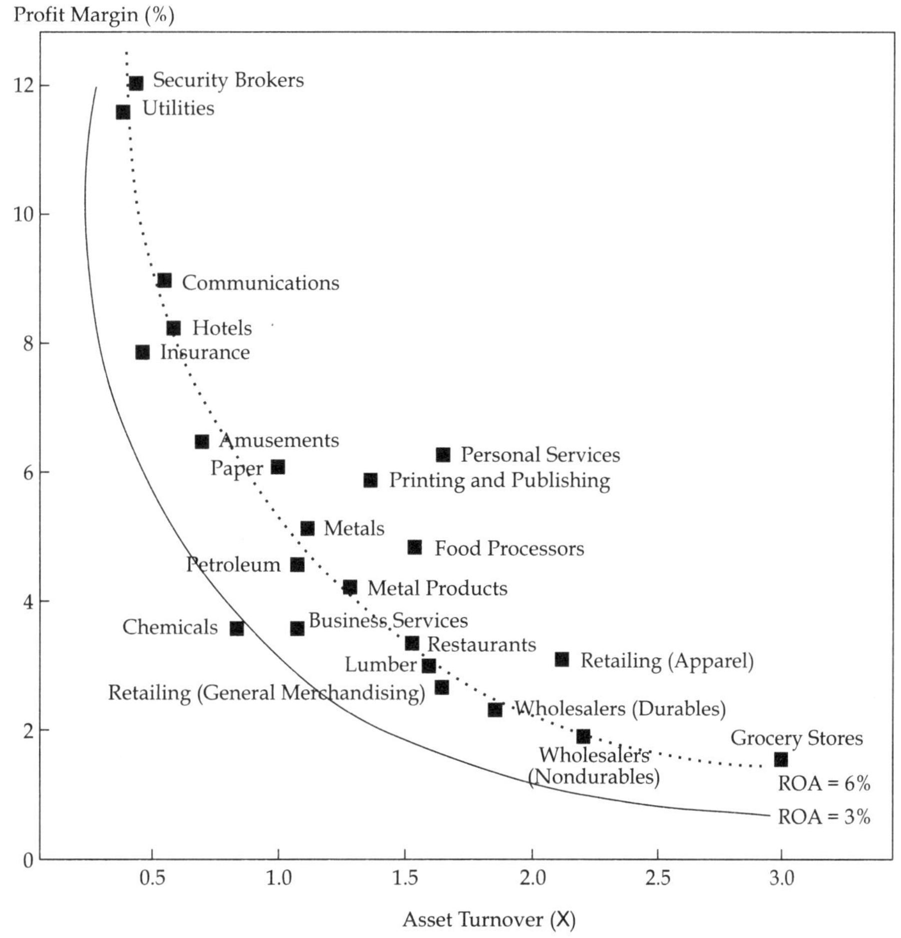

Source: Based on data from Stickney and Brown (1999).

Table 2. Average Annual Median Profit Margin, Asset Turnover, and ROA for Selected Industries, 1987–96

Industry/Sector	Profit Margin	Asset Turnover	ROA
Forest products industry			
Lumber	3.1%	1.56	5.9%
Paper processing	6.1	1.12	6.9
Printing and publishing	6.1	1.21	7.5
Apparel industry			
Textile manufacturing	4.3	1.45	6.1
Apparel manufacturing	3.9	1.74	6.4
Apparel retailing	3.1	2.26	6.9
Food industry			
Food processors	4.7	1.48	7.2
Grocery stores	1.9	3.27	6.3
Restaurants	3.3	1.53	5.4

Figure 2 and Table 2; obviously, they should look at the individual measures for a company. The point is that, even though analysts should evaluate ROA, profit margin, and asset turnover at the individual level, analysts can start at the aggregate level, get characteristics of the industry and sectors of the industry, and then deal with company-specific information.

Understanding and Cleansing the Financial Statements

Understanding and cleansing the financial statements (step three) is done at the company-specific level. To say anything about how the numbers should be cleansed (how they should be restated), the analyst must understand the context in which the numbers were generated, which goes back to understanding the key characteristics of the company and the industry. This section discusses earnings management as one of the main reasons for cleansing financial statements and shows how analysis of the Coca-Cola Company benefits from such cleansing.

Earnings Management. Because earnings play such a central role in most analyses, the analyst needs to be alert to the possibility that reported earnings, for a particular quarter or year, may be a poor predictor of ongoing profitability. One of the primary causes of the discrepancy between current and future profitability is the bias that results from management's efforts to look better, primarily by managing earnings. Analysts need to determine how meaningful the earnings numbers reported by management are.

Because assessing the sustainability of earnings is key, understanding earnings management practices is vital. Earnings management is practiced in overt and some less-than-overt ways. Among the most fertile ground for earnings management is the treatment of nonrecurring or unusual items, and the issue is whether the effect this treatment has on earnings is transitory or permanent. The following five examples, which are by no means an exhaustive list, highlight five areas of potential earnings distortion.

■ *Discontinued operations*. If a company decides to exit a particular segment of its business, it must report separate disclosures related to that business. How the company reports the gain/loss on the transaction—when it is reported, how it is measured, even whether it is a gain or loss—involves a great degree of subjectivity.

■ *Changes in accounting principles*. The FASB is constantly issuing new standards, and many of these standards require changes on income statements. In fact, one of the most recent changes is related to a concept called "comprehensive income." Analysts should be thinking about whether and how they will use this comprehensive income number, which most corporations will now report. In addition to FASB-induced changes, companies also change accounting principles voluntarily, a phenomenon that is potentially distortive and even harder to assess than more broadly applied FASB-induced changes.

■ *Impairment losses*. Companies must disclose and write down asset values when they *anticipate* that assets previously acquired will no longer provide future benefits. This disclosure is quite useful, particularly if it is analyzed in the context of a past strategic decision by a company. If a company decided four years ago to buy a particular division of another company and then three and a half years later the company takes an impairment write-down for those assets, the company is confessing to a strategic decision that did not work. The company is required to report the write-down, but deciding when to report and how to measure the write-down is subjective.

■ *Restructuring charges*. Companies frequently will not get out of a business, which would be a discontinued operation, but rather will stay in the particular business and make changes in the strategic direction or level of operations. These changes are inevitably accompanied by a plethora of "restructuring charges," a practice that is now probably the most frequently occurring abuse in financial reporting.

■ *Changes of estimates.* Changes of estimates could be seen as an example related to restructuring, but it is a more generic phenomenon. Estimates, and changes in those estimates, are a part of depreciation charges, debt reserves, and warranties, to name only a few among many such items.

To give just one illustration of how pervasive changes in estimates are, the SEC recently asked SunTrust Bank to restate its reserves because the bank, in order to reserve funds for future weak periods, had estimated bigger reserves than it currently needed. Lowering reserves by $100 million increased earnings, net of taxes, more than $60 million. Restating reserves had the effect of increasing the earnings of SunTrust. Clearly the bank's profitability had not changed in the least.

The lesson is that subjectivity is the name of the game in most financial reporting areas. Analysts, therefore, must cleanse and restate the numbers if they are going to do effective time-series and cross-sectional analysis.

Cleansing Example. The Coca-Cola Company has developed a particular strategy for operating its bottling operations. Most of its concentrate in syrup is bottled by companies that are only minority owned by Coca-Cola. In other words, Coca-Cola does not bottle most of its products. In fact, for those companies in which Coca-Cola owns less than 20 percent of the stock, investments in these companies are simply recorded as any other stock investment. But for those companies in which Coca-Cola owns 20–50 percent of the stock—Coca-Cola Enterprises and Coca-Cola Amatil are the most obvious examples—those investments are reported using the so-called equity method. **Table 3** shows the results of cleansing Coca-Cola's financial statements as if the company had consolidated all of its equity affiliates, which one could argue Coca-Cola should do because it effectively has control over all these affiliates. The "Eliminations" column shows the cleansing adjustments needed to achieve consolidated presentation. If Coca-Cola did this type of consolidation, the "Consolidated" column of Table 3 shows that the company would have reported total assets of more than $40 billion, compared with the actual reported total assets of $16 billion shown in the unconsolidated Coca-Cola Company column of Table 3.

Table 3. Coca-Cola Company and Equity Method Affiliates Consolidation Worksheet, December 31, 1996 (US$ millions)

Line Item	Coca-Cola Company	Coca-Cola Enterprises	Coca-Cola Amatil	Other Equity Investments	Eliminations		Consolidated
Current assets	$ 5,910	$ 1,319	$1,847	$ 2,792			$11,868
Investments in securities	5,948	—	—		(A)	$ –547[a]	
					(B)	–881[a]	
					(C)	–2,004[a]	2,516
Noncurrent assets	4,303	9,915	2,913	8,783	(A)	–151[b]	
					(B)	+137[c]	
					(C)	+583[d]	26,484
Total assets	$16,161	$11,234	$4,760	$11,575			$40,868
Current liabilities	$ 7,406	$ 1,390	$1,247	$ 2,758			$12,801
Noncurrent liabilities	2,599	8,294	1,445	4,849			17,187
External interests	—	—	—	—	(A)	+853[e]	
					(B)	+1,324[f]	
					(C)	+2,547[g]	4,724
Shareholders' equity	$ 6,156	$ 1,550	$2,068	$ 3,968	(A)	–1,550[a]	
					(B)	–2,068[a]	
					(C)	–3,968[a]	6,156
Total liabilities and equity	$16,161	$11,234	$4,760	$11,575			$40,868

[a] Given in Coke's Note 3.
[b] –$151 = [$547 – (0.45 × $1,550)].
[c] $137 = [$881 – (0.36 × $2,068)].
[d] $583 = [$2,004 – (0.358 × $3,968)].
[e] $853 = 0.55 × $1,550.
[f] $1,324 = 0.64 × $2,068.
[g] $2,547 = (1 – 0.0358) × $3,968.

The truth of the matter is that the amount of assets that Coca-Cola effectively has under its control is not $16 billion but more than $40 billion. The 1996 ROA for Coca-Cola Company was 24 percent based on the actual numbers; it would have been about 12.5 percent based on these *pro forma* numbers. Coca-Cola did nothing wrong here. It did not violate generally accepted accounting principles, but its reported ROA would drop by more than half if it had done this cleansing. The FASB is looking into requiring this type of reporting for any company that has effective control of its affiliates, regardless of the percentage of ownership.

R&D Disclosures

The area of R&D reporting and disclosures is now one of the most egregious areas for reporting failure—so much so that it warrants separate discussion. Even most policy makers (the SEC and the FASB) are signaling that the reporting problems in the area of R&D are to the point at which the disclosures are probably misleading. R&D disclosures are, in a word, poor, and R&D-based valuations are, therefore, suspect at best.

The basic rule (FASB Statement No. 2), which came out in 1974, is that R&D costs must be expensed as incurred. The basis for FASB Statement No. 2 was the type of R&D work conducted by the National Science Foundation, defense contractors, and the large pharmaceutical companies, which is a very different type of R&D activity in very different industries than exist now. In 1974, the emphasis was not on biotechnology or telecommunications companies, simply because those were not the dominant companies.

Many different models are used to value R&D, and they all are incredibly imprecise. They usually start with an estimate of the completion of technology, how much cost is needed to complete the technology, and estimates by product categories of future revenue streams from the technology. So, the models are revenue-stream based. Companies follow no specific rules in making these R&D valuation calculations. Auditors are not voicing an opinion as to the value that is put on the R&D; they are, however, giving opinions as to the reasonableness of the assumptions that went into the model, so there is a degree of accountability for these values. What is important about having adequate disclosure is not the following of rules but providing the input for the valuation model, whatever model is used.

Estimating R&D costs is an important part of the valuation process, and such costs can be valued using either an indirect or direct method. The work being done by Lev and Sougiannis (1996), in which they try to value past R&D expenditures relative to revenue streams, exemplifies the indirect method. Specifically, they have related R&D expenditures in one year to revenues of subsequent years, because in theory at least, the purpose of R&D expenditures is to generate revenues in future years. What they found is that R&D expenditures generate clear benefits for five to nine years from the time the expenditures are incurred. Lev and Sougiannis are currently working on valuing R&D and pegging it directly to stock price movement. Their work is probably the closest anyone has come to valuing soft assets.

The direct method involves looking at a company's R&D disclosures under the assumption that these disclosures are accurate. The problem is that some companies are reporting R&D expenditures of 10–60 percent of revenues without anything that approximates appropriate disclosure. Such expense levels and amounts are clearly important, but the disclosures are either nonexistent or not relevant.

A particularly noteworthy example of adequate R&D disclosure, and of the possibilities of the direct method, relates to the purchase method in a business combination. Purchased in-process R&D is a form of R&D cost that shows up only in one situation: when one company buys another company in a purchase, rather than pooling, transaction. In the past, for instance, when America Online bought companies using the purchase method, it generated and immediately wrote off this asset (i.e., purchased in-process R&D), sometimes to the tune of 50–60 percent of the cost of the deal. The positive aspect of this phenomenon is that, under the purchase method, a company must disclose the fair value of its R&D expenditures. These disclosures give an analyst tremendous fodder to discuss how management assessed these values and to work directly with the companies to determine the added value. Thus, under the purchase method, direct values of R&D are being produced.

In fact, the SEC requires companies to report these fair-value disclosures in the purchase method situation and to disclose the following types of information: how the valuation is arrived at; what valuation technique was used; if the technology is written off, whether or not the company will develop it; and some description of the company's intentions with this acquired technology.

Many companies are on the verge of voluntary disclosures as well. Indeed, companies themselves will have to think about better R&D disclosures. Every company that buys another company with the purchase method is under increasing pressure to state what it is writing off and how it valued the write-offs, in particular, R&D disclosures. Companies are reluctantly but surely providing the information, and a company's reluctance to provide information is a good sign that the information is important.

Conclusion

Analysts clearly need help in the area of better financial reporting and disclosure. Without question, the reporting system as it stands now has major flaws. Regulators, users of the data, and academics must push companies further in terms of reporting and disclosure, especially in key areas such as R&D disclosures.

Ultimately and fortunately, market forces are likely to drive companies to do their own cleansing and to disclose necessary and relevant information. Holders of large stock positions in some cases have already assumed the role of "heavy hitter," going after a corporation for better disclosures; other major stakeholders can and will do likewise. The SEC has in fact given them the ability to pressure corporations along exactly those lines. All these forces together should work to produce a reporting system that is at least marginally better than the one in place now.

Question and Answer Session

Paul R. Brown

Question: How should analysts take into account the executive stock options that have become a significant "nonexpense expense" for some companies, such as Microsoft Corporation?

Brown: There is ongoing debate about whether we can value these stock options, but the FASB's failure in this area was political, not substantive. In fact, there is no question that we can value these options, and the *pro forma* footnotes for most corporations provide disclosure of these option positions. This disclosure is based on the materiality threshold of what a company's EPS and diluted EPS would be if these options were taken into consideration. Coca-Cola has this disclosure, with a recent EPS effect of a couple of cents. For some high-tech companies, the effect is more like 40 or 50 percent on the reported earnings.

So, I recommend working with the *pro forma* disclosures, which treat stock options as if they were an expense on the income statement. Of course, subjectivity is involved, but these values are no more subjective than are any of the other subjective areas of financial reporting.

Question: What should analysts look for in footnotes on derivatives?

Brown: The new disclosures on derivatives will first appear in quarterly reports in 2001. Certain derivatives will have substantial income statement effects. For these derivatives, the changes in their fair value will be reported in "comprehensive income," which is not on the income statement. I would look at the volatility in the valuations of the derivatives from quarter to quarter. For most derivatives, the changes in their values are not going to hit the income statement but are going to go directly to shareholders' equity.

Question: How do analysts account for a case in which a company makes an acquisition, writes off $X million, and declares the acquisition additive?

Brown: The write-off could belong to many categories, but it is probably purchased in-process R&D. The acquisition must have value or they would not have paid for it. You cannot write off goodwill immediately, and the same goes for brand names or customer satisfaction. So, the value must be in some asset that has not yet reached fruition. The first thing that I would do is look at the specific categories of the write-offs; in my opinion, a substantial if not total portion of the write-off will fall in the category of "purchased in-process R&D."

Cross-Border Financial Statement Analysis

Gary S. Schieneman
Vice President, Comparative Global Equity Analysis
Merrill Lynch & Company, Inc.

> Cross-border accounting differences that exist among countries can greatly complicate the task of analyzing financial statements. In particular, variations in treatment of goodwill and taxes can distort the results of traditional valuation measures. With harmonization of accounting methods unlikely in the near future, global equity analysts need to know the accounting story behind financial statements and need to make appropriate adjustments to accommodate the value-specific effects of differing accounting treatments.

Accounting, by its very nature, presents problems for cross-border financial statement analysis. First, accounting does not travel well, but it was never intended to. Accounting got its start to satisfy tax collectors and legal requirements; the needs of a capital market were never important in the development of accounting. Until the 1990s, capital markets had little impact on the development of accounting, except in the United States and some English-speaking countries. So, the fact that cross-border differences exist in accounting is not surprising.

Second, no "truth" exists in accounting. No one system is inherently better than another system. Although global harmonization of accounting may increase, the world is unlikely to accept U.S. generally accepted accounting principles (GAAP) as the basis for a global accounting system. The U.S. SEC's mandated disclosures are, in my opinion, better than any other system worldwide, but the information contained in the basic financial statements and footnotes is not necessarily superior to many other systems.

Third, although accounting appears to be precise, it is not. The detailed rules contained in Financial Accounting Standards Board (FASB) opinions enhance this impression of precision. Unfortunately, many companies look at how to get around the rules rather than how to present useful information. Almost all the data included in financial statements are based on subjective decisions and could be presented differently. Quarterly reporting increases the difficulty of preparing financial information with any degree of accuracy.

Finally, the manner in which the score is kept (financial reporting) influences the decision-making process. For example, the United Kingdom's more permissive accounting for mergers and acquisitions and goodwill has tended to encourage more acquisitions in the United Kingdom than in other countries. Because of this permissiveness, U.K. companies, in my view, have tended to overpay for acquisitions compared with companies in other countries in which the accounting rules are more rigid.

Global markets need more harmonization of accounting than currently exists. As users of financial accounting information begin to look at stocks on a global basis, the consistency of the numbers becomes more important. As this trend accelerates, the demand for harmonization will increase even more. The biggest problem with differences in accounting between countries is when people use information on a macro basis without understanding the nature of the information and the extent to which the numbers are different. For example, a market's P/E could change if a country changed accounting rules that resulted in different earnings being reported. To say that Hong Kong is cheap and Germany is expensive does not mean much without understanding that accounting differences affect their relative cheapness and expensiveness.

This presentation discusses how accounting differences between countries affect the way analysts look at companies and markets. It also comments on some approaches to valuation and how well they work for cross-border comparisons.

©2000, Association for Investment Management and Research

Effects of Differences: Companies

Accounting differences affect how analysts look at companies. Differing accounting practices between countries or differing accounting practices within a country because of rule changes can significantly alter the results of the valuation process. For example, the FASB has attempted to impose requirements that would value stock options and report them as part of compensation expense. If companies that use options as a major compensation element were to impute a value to stock options, they would report sharply lower earnings. In the United States, companies in the technology sector use options extensively. I estimate that imputing a value to those options in 1998 would have reduced earnings for this sector by 20 percent, with greater reductions in sectors with little or no profit, such as Internet companies. Because companies do not like to see their earnings reduced, nobody is imputing a value to stock options.

Stock valuation is dependent on the information available. Differences in accounting can produce significantly different relative valuations for comparable companies. Goodwill is a particularly important difference.

The following discussion of goodwill and the company-specific examples show the effect of differing accounting practices on company valuation.

Comparative Goodwill. With the 40-year amortization period used by most U.S. companies, goodwill amortization in the United States historically has not been particularly onerous. This view is not true for acquisitions by technology and drug companies, for which the major part of the purchase price is allocated to intangibles. For countries following international standards or in the United Kingdom, where a 20-year amortization is now the rule, the amortization of goodwill has a far greater impact than it does for U.S. companies.

The FASB is revisiting the subject of goodwill and the issue of purchase versus pooling accounting. With respect to goodwill, the FASB has tentatively agreed to limit the write-off period to a maximum of 20 years. A 20-year write-off period will have a substantial impact on many U.S. companies.

To understand the potential significance of changing to a 20-year period for goodwill, consider the example of U.S. and U.K. drug companies, as shown in **Table 1**. Clearly, goodwill is a major part of the assets of these companies. The companies most affected by the change would be Pharmacia & Upjohn and Warner-Lambert, and with a 20-year write-off, the goodwill of Merck would be approaching 10 percent, which is substantial.

There is no right or wrong way to account for goodwill. Present practice is to capitalize and amortize goodwill or, alternatively, to write it off directly against shareholders' equity, which was the policy in the United Kingdom up to 1998. The trend among accountants is to opt for the former. Recently, the United Kingdom issued a new standard that requires capitalization and amortization. The period of amortization will be a 20-year maximum, which is the same for the rest of the world, except the United States. However, if a company can show that the goodwill has a longer life, it can use a longer period. Alternatively, if a company can show that the goodwill has an indefinite life, it can choose not to amortize the goodwill and leave it in the balance sheet indefinitely as an asset.

When the U.K. opinion was first issued, I assumed that most companies would opt for the indefinite-life approach because it would give companies the best of both worlds. U.K. companies could increase assets and equity without penalizing future earnings. In practice, however, most companies have opted for a 20-year amortization period.

Table 1. Comparative Goodwill Accounts for U.S. and U.K. Companies

Company	Goodwill Assets	Goodwill Equity	Reduction in Income/Goodwill Amortization 20 Years	Reduction in Income/Goodwill Amortization 40 Years
U.S. companies				
Bristol-Myers Squibb	10.8%	22.5%	2.5%	1.3%
Eli Lilly	6.5	35.9	4.0	2.0
Merck	29.4	60.2	7.9	3.9
Pfizer	9.4	18.2	3.2	1.6
Pharmacia & Upjohn	11.7	21.9	15.9	7.9
Warner-Lambert	23.3	65.9	10.2	5.1
U.K. companies				
Glaxo Wellcome	47.7	80.7	20.1	10.4
SmithKline Beecham	48.6	171.0	21.8	10.9

The explanation for the companies' surprising decision to amortize involves the adoption of the opinion. The U.K. standard-setting board permitted either retroactive or prospective adoption. The board encouraged retroactive adoption but did not require it. Under retroactive adoption, a company would restate all the prior periods for the goodwill that was written off and for amortization that would have reduced earnings in these years. Almost all companies have not elected retroactive adoption. Rather, they have chosen prospective adoption, beginning with 1998 transactions. The result is that U.K. accounting will have no consistency for a number of years, and this inconsistency could last as long as 20 years, depending on when a company made its last major acquisition before the new opinion. U.K. accounting, therefore, will continue to be out of line with U.S. accounting and with that of other countries that require capitalization and amortization.

The International Accounting Standards Committee (IASC) issued a revised standard on goodwill that became effective beginning in 1995. This revised standard also requires capitalization and amortization over a maximum 20-year period. Once again, this new requirement has been adopted prospectively and major inconsistencies will continue to exist for past goodwill.

Although accountants around the world now agree that goodwill should be capitalized and amortized, excluding goodwill as an expense penalizes companies that grow organically. Growth via acquisition appears more desirable when a significant cost element is ignored for determining postacquisition profits. If analysts ignore goodwill from the expense side, they should pay more attention to profitability rather than profits. This includes return on assets and invested capital, which is adjusted to include the total cost of acquisitions. If the company overpays for the earnings growth generated by acquisitions, relatively low returns on assets and capital should reflect this fact.

Glaxo Wellcome. The valuation for Glaxo Wellcome, a large British drug company, varies depending on whether the analyst uses U.K. or U.S. GAAP. Glaxo acquired Wellcome for about £9 billion. More than £7 billion of the purchase price was for intangibles. In the drug sector, intangibles are the primary asset acquired in an acquisition—mainly patents covering the existing products or amounts expended for research in the pipeline. At the time of the Wellcome acquisition, the predominant practice in the United Kingdom was to write off goodwill immediately against shareholders' equity and not treat it as an expense. If Glaxo had been a U.S. company, Glaxo would have had to capitalize the good-

Table 2. Glaxo Wellcome: Comparative 1997 Earnings
(£ in millions)

U.K. GAAP	
Net income	1,850[a]
U.S. GAAP adjustments	
Goodwill amortization	(554)
Intangible amortization	(326)
Deferred tax	(31)
Other	13[b]
Net income	952
Percent decrease	(48.5%)
Shareholders' equity	
U.K. GAAP	1,843
U.S. GAAP	7,882
Percent increase	327.6%

[a]£0.52 per share.
[b]£0.26 per share.

will and write it off over time. **Table 2** shows data from Glaxo's Form 20f, in which Glaxo adopted a 10-year amortization period for its goodwill. This period is much closer to reality than the maximum 40-year period that U.S. GAAP permits. As a result of amortizing goodwill and other intangibles that were written off under U.K. GAAP, the company's earnings dropped almost 50 percent.

On a U.K. GAAP basis, Glaxo trades at about 44 times trailing earnings and thus is similar to Merck and Bristol Myers but much cheaper than Pfizer and Warner Lambert on a trailing earnings basis. On a U.S. GAAP basis, however, Glaxo trades at 88 times trailing earnings, making it one of the most expensive drug stocks we follow. The question is whether Glaxo is reasonably priced or expensive.

Because of the immediate write-off of goodwill, big problems also exist when one looks at shareholders' equity. At the end of 1997, Glaxo's equity was about £1.8 billion on a U.K. basis and £7.9 billion on a U.S. GAAP basis. On a reported basis, U.K. companies tend to have astounding rates of return on equity. Unless analysts adjust shareholders' equity for the differences in accounting, these high rates of return do not mean anything. With Glaxo, the adjustment increases equity by almost 328 percent.

LVMH. LVMH Moët Hennessy Louis Vuitton's net income for 1995–1997 varies significantly depending on whether French or U.S. GAAP is used, as shown in **Table 3**. The major U.S. GAAP adjustments are interesting. Brand amortization is the largest recurring difference. In France and some other countries (including the United Kingdom and Australia), accountants can separate brand valuation from goodwill. Once brand names have been recog-

Table 3. LVMH: Comparative Net Income
(FFr in millions)

Line Item	1995	1996	1997
French GAAP			
Net income	4,047	3,683	4,528
U.S. GAAP adjustments			
Unrealized gain (loss) on marketable securities	22	(46)	6
Write-down of treasury stock			33
Goodwill amortization	(8)	(7)	(8)
Brand amortization	(233)	(21)	(152)
Foreign exchange hedges	307	(287)	(85)
Bonds with warrants	(45)	(45)	—
Acquisition accounting	—	(954)	—
Reorganization costs			1,841
Translation	12	49	(68)
Net income	4,102	2,372	6,095
Percent change	1.4%	(35.6%)	34.6%

nized in the balance sheet, amortization is not required except for a diminution in value, which I have never seen in practice. The brand names for LVMH are recorded at their acquisition values, and no amortization occurs. Under U.S. GAAP, there is no distinction between brand names and goodwill, and both are subject to amortization as part of goodwill.

A second large adjustment concerns foreign exchange hedging. Many companies use foreign exchange forward contracts to hedge future cash flows, future purchase commitments, future dividend remittances, and so on. Throughout the world, companies typically use hedge accounting for these contracts. Under hedge accounting, unrealized gain or loss on the open contract is deferred until the transaction occurs and the hedge is closed.

Under present U.S. GAAP, companies cannot use hedge contract accounting for these particular hedges. Instead, U.S. GAAP considers them speculative hedges and requires mark-to-market accounting. The company's income reflects any unrealized gain or loss. Hedging is an important item for companies outside the United States, where many dollar-denominated transactions exist. Because of the U.S. accounting approach and marking to market, analysts have no way to anticipate the effect of hedging on the profit and loss statement, which can be huge for some companies. This difference will disappear by 2001 when the United States implements the new derivatives accounting requirements.

Another large adjustment involves assets transferred among related entities. LVMH valued these at market prices and recognized gains. Under U.S. GAAP, the transactions should be valued at book value similar to pooling-of-interest accounting.

Another major difference applies to restructuring costs. Under U.S. GAAP, restrictive criteria exist for when a company can reflect a provision for restructuring costs. Such restrictive criteria do not exist outside the United States. Non-U.S. companies normally recognize restructuring provisions earlier than U.S. companies.

Nestlé. People often perceive the Swiss as being very conservative. This perception is not true and could limit the usefulness of Swiss financial information. In fact, the major companies in Switzerland now use international accounting standards for shareholder reporting. The only Swiss accounting requirements concern the local statutory accounts, which are of little interest to investors.

In 1997, Nestlé reported income of about SFr4 billion, as shown in **Table 4**. On a U.S. GAAP basis, the company's earnings were only 4 percent lower than what it reported. The composition of the adjustments shown in Table 4 destroys the notion of conservatism in Switzerland.

Table 4. Nestlé: 1997 Earnings
(SFr in millions)

Swiss GAAP	
Reported net income	4,005
Estimated U.S. GAAP adjustments	
Goodwill	(330)
Current value depreciation	245
Deferred tax	(75)
Hedging	(10)
Pensions	NA
Net income	3,835
Percent change	(4.2%)

NA = not available.

■ *Goodwill.* Goodwill is the major accounting difference when adjusting to U.S. GAAP. Nestlé, which follows international accounting standards, wrote off goodwill immediately against retained earnings through 1994. In 1995, the revised international standard abolished immediate write-off, and companies had to capitalize and amortize goodwill. Swiss companies adopted the opinion prospectively. My estimated U.S. GAAP adjustment is based on goodwill write-offs dating back to the mid 1980s. The SFr330 million charge against earnings in Table 4 represents amortization on a 20-year basis, which is the criterion Nestlé now uses for post-1994 transactions.

■ *Current value depreciation.* In the mid-1980s, Nestlé made several large acquisitions that resulted in significant goodwill write-offs against equity. To reinstate this equity, Nestlé did not adjust its goodwill accounting but rather started writing up fixed assets to current value. The revalued amounts were the basis for depreciation expense. Under U.S. GAAP, fixed asset revaluation is not permissible and depreciation on revaluation must be reversed.

■ *Deferred tax.* Nestlé uses a partial allocation approach for deferring taxes. If timing differences between book and tax will likely not result in future taxes payable or recoverable, no deferred taxes are provided. In the United States and many other countries, deferred taxes are provided on all differences between book and tax—the so-called "comprehensive" method of allocation. In my opinion, the partial approach is closer to reality but it is more subjective and subject to manipulation than the comprehensive approach.

■ *Hedging.* For hedging, the adjustment to U.S. GAAP was based on amounts Nestlé disclosed in its annual report.

■ *Pensions.* Pension amounts are not available at Nestlé. Pensions are a major accounting difference that analysts should consider when they examine companies on a cross-border basis. Unfortunately, analysts cannot determine with any degree of precision what the right pension charge should be for Nestlé because the company operates worldwide and has a number of pension plans.

Effects of Differences: Markets

In addition to affecting fundamental analysis, accounting differences also affect comparative market valuation, which has an impact on asset allocation.

Multiples. Table 5 shows P/E multiples and price-to-cash earnings (P/CE) ratios, which is earnings plus depreciation, for 10 markets. On a P/E basis, Hong Kong appears to be the cheapest market and Japan, the United States, and Switzerland the most expensive. But are these markets as cheap or expensive as they look?

A number of factors affect relative market valuation. One item to consider is the composition of the market. The markets shown in Table 5 are not comparable. For example, markets in Australia and Canada consist largely of extraction-oriented industries. Germany's orientation is toward heavy manufacturing, and its market index includes a number of conglomerates. Hong Kong is heavily weighted toward the property sector. Food and drug companies compose the bulk of the Swiss market capitalization, and financial services dominate in the United Kingdom.

Accounting differences are another item to consider. If the EPS data used for P/E purposes in Table 5 were adjusted to a U.S. GAAP basis of accounting, the multiples would increase for most of these markets. In relation to the United States, these markets are not as cheap as they appear to be.

As Table 5 shows, Hong Kong looks cheap on a P/E basis but expensive on a P/CE basis. Many

Table 5. Global Valuations Based on P/E and P/CE, as of November 30, 1998

Country	Multiple P/E	Multiple P/CE	Rank P/E	Rank P/CE	U.S. GAAP: Increase or Decrease in Multiple
Australia	19.7	11.6	3	6	Increase
Canada	22.4	9.8	5	2	Increase
France	25.5	11.0	7	5	—
Germany	23.4	8.8	6	1	Decrease
Hong Kong	18.1	13.7	1	8	Increase
Japan	191.0	10.1	10	3	—
Netherlands	19.6	11.0	2	4	Increase
Switzerland	28.0	18.8	8	10	Increase
United Kingdom	20.0	13.2	4	7	Increase
United States	28.5	17.0	9	9	na

na = not applicable.

Note: A dash in the last column signifies that there was no significant increase or decrease.

Source: Morgan Stanley Capital International (MSCI).

analysts favor cash as a basis for eliminating these accounting differences, but keep in mind that P/CE is not cash but income plus depreciation. Hong Kong is relatively expensive on a P/CE basis because of the way the property sector accounts for rental properties. Rather than depreciate these assets, Hong Kong has adopted the U.K. approach of revaluing rental properties annually. As long as the assets increase in value, there is no charge against earnings.

The property sector for Hong Kong is somewhat similar to a real estate investment trust in the United States. When looking at REITs, nobody cares about depreciation because cash flow is the most important consideration. Hong Kong market earnings are much closer to cash flow than are those in other markets. Because Hong Kong is so different in that respect, the only way analysts can say that Hong Kong is cheap or expensive is in relation to its past, not in comparison with other markets.

Germany and Japan look expensive on a P/E basis, but on a cash earnings basis, they look cheap. In my opinion, low P/CE multiples do not represent cheapness but rather reflect depreciation attributable to overinvestment. This overinvestment has been caused in part by high tax rates and low cost of capital in both countries.

Reported Earnings versus U.S. GAAP. I adjusted the reported earnings for nine European countries to U.S. GAAP, as shown in **Table 6**. With the exception of Switzerland and Germany, for which I made my own adjustments, this project was essentially a compilation. The study was based on companies that were included in the MSCI index for each country and that listed their stocks in the United States. Listed companies must file an annual Form 20F report, which is similar to the 10K required for U.S. companies. The 20F requirements include a U.S. GAAP reconciliation, which was the basis for this study. The percentage of MSCI income captured in the study ranged from about 50 percent for the United Kingdom to 95 percent for the Netherlands. The sample, therefore, seems reasonably representative.

Table 6 shows that accounting differences are not so great at the market level. The market with the most overstated earnings is the United Kingdom, followed by Switzerland. The two countries with the most understated earnings are Spain and Germany.

■ *France.* In France, the huge overstatement was the result of a one-time reversal of pension reserves at France Télécom pursuant to privatization. The provisions were never acceptable under U.S. GAAP, and the adjustment eliminates the profit resulting from reversal. Excluding one-time items, no difference exists between French reported earnings and U.S. GAAP. This conclusion is based on an average of all the French companies in the study, including LVMH.

■ *Germany.* Germany is the most interesting of the nine countries examined in the study. German financial reporting is conventionally viewed as ultra conservative and not very useful. The study's findings contradict this view. The 16 companies in the study, all of which were components of the DAX 30, showed little difference between net income under German GAAP and net income under U.S. GAAP.

Germany's 6.1 percent understatement largely stemmed from Volkswagen and two insurance companies (Allianz Group and Munich Reinsurance Company). Volkswagen's earnings have historically been understated because of provisioning for future losses. Insurance reporting throughout Europe is oriented toward regulators, and earnings are lower than would be reported under U.S. GAAP. Without VW and the insurance companies, virtually no difference exists between reported earnings under the DVFA (Deutsche Vereingung für Finanzanalyse und Anlageberatung) method—used for EPS purposes and reported earnings—and under U.S. GAAP.

The DVFA is the German society of security analysts. It has an approach for adjusting reported earnings to increase them to a level that my work indicates is a reasonable proxy for U.S. GAAP. The adjustments include elimination of changes in long-term reserves charged against income. Provisioning is a major difference between German and U.S. GAAP. Under German GAAP, provisions are made for future losses that are not only possible but probable—a big difference. The DVFA approach also adds back goodwill amortization (this requirement has subsequently been abolished), asset write-downs, and extraordinary depreciation. As a result, the EPS of a German company is not based on reported earnings and is not as understated as some think.

Table 6. Reported Earnings versus U.S. GAAP, 1995–97

Country	Recurring Adjustments	Total Change in Income
France	–0.9%	33.4%
Germany	–6.1	–4.5
Ireland	1.8	–1.6
Italy	2.5	–3.5
Netherlands	2.7	2.5
Spain	–7.6	–15.9
Sweden	–4.8	–4.4
Switzerland	8.6	8.6
United Kingdom	12.9	12.1

Note: Negative numbers are understated reported earnings versus U.S. GAAP, and positive numbers are overstated earnings versus U.S. GAAP.

A number of large German companies use international standards for consolidated financial reporting, and more are expected to adopt them in the future. This trend should further alleviate concerns about German financial reporting.

■ *Spain*. Several factors, including goodwill and deferred taxes, caused the understatement in Spain. Goodwill was capitalized in Spain but was written off over 10 years, the maximum period. Thus, the write-off period was much shorter than would be used under U.S. GAAP. Extending the write-off period would have increased earnings for Spain.

■ *Switzerland*. The overstatement of earnings in Switzerland largely resulted from goodwill arising prior to 1995, when the international standard was revised. In Switzerland, as in the United Kingdom, writing off goodwill resulted in overstating earnings and understating the market multiple.

■ *United Kingdom*. In the United Kingdom, the overstatement of U.K. earnings and the relative understatement of the market multiple were almost entirely the result of goodwill accounting. Many other differences exist, but they tend to offset each other and are unimportant overall.

Tax Considerations. When making global valuations, analysts often overlook taxes because of the complexity. **Table 7** is a summary of effective tax rates for U.S. and non-U.S. companies in the technology sector. Effective tax rates in the United States are similar to the statutory rate because of comprehensive deferred tax accounting. For a U.S. company, the tax rate is 35 percent, and any difference is the result of having foreign subsidiaries or substantial operating losses that could not be recognized under U.S. GAAP.

Outside the United States, a wide range of tax rates exists. In many countries, the statutory rate is lower than that in the United States. Most of the Southeast Asian countries and Taiwan and South Korea grant incentives, such as tax holidays or tax credits, for investments in technology. This practice brings the effective rate for Asian companies to a low level. Germany and Japan are high-tax countries. Tax reduction is slated to begin in Japan in fiscal 1999, and proposals have been made to reduce German rates.

■ *Germany*. In Germany, the average overall effective tax rate in company financial statements is about 55 percent, the maximum statutory rate for undistributed earnings. The rate on distributed earnings is about 40 percent. If the effective rate were 35 percent (the average U.S. rate), German earnings would go up by 40–45 percent and Germany would be one of the cheapest markets in the world. Part of the reason for the high German effective rate is accounting. At the present time, German GAAP

Table 7. Technology Sector: Effective Tax Rates

Company	U.S. Rate	Non-U.S. Rate
Software		
Baan (Netherlands)		31.9%
Computer Associates International	37.6%	
Microsoft Corporation	35.0	
Oracle Corporation	–2.3	
SAP (Germany)		44.5
Semiconductor		
Intel Corporation	34.8	
Kyocera Corporation (Japan)		57.8
Macronix International (Taiwan)		–77.7
National Semiconductor Corporation	23.1	
STMicroelectronics (France)		21.9
Texas Instruments	35.0	
Computers/PC		
Acer (Taiwan)		–4.9
Compaq	32.7	
Dell Computer Corporation	31.0	
Hewlett-Packard	30.0	
IBM Corporation	32.5	
Communications		
Alcatel (France)		24.2
Cisco Systems	35.1	
Ericsson (Sweden)		30.6
Lucent Technologies	37.1	
Motorola	35.0	
Nokia Corporation (Finland)		27.2
Nortel Networks (Canada)		34.6
Electronic equipment		
NEC Corporation (Japan)		52.7
Average	33.4%	22.1%

requires deferred tax liabilities to be recognized but not deferred tax assets. Adoption of international standards should lead to a reduction in deferred tax expense as the assets are recognized.

In Germany, high tax rates and low cost of capital attributable to unfunded pension liabilities make capital investment appear more profitable than would be the case in other countries. Although pension liabilities are unfunded, German companies get a tax deduction for making a bookkeeping entry debiting pension expense and crediting the liability. In other countries, funding is required and is the basis for tax deductions. The unfunded pensions have been a major source of capital for German companies. Although German pension accounting has an interest element (pension expense is based on change in the liability, which is a discounted amount), no out-of-pocket cost is associated with it.

Many German companies have substantial marketable security portfolios that are in part pension fund assets. These portfolios vary among companies depending on their financing needs. For example, a large part of Volkswagen's liability is invested in the company, so the workers must look to VW's cash flow as the primary source of pension payments. As the workforce ages and pensions become a real expense, pensions will be an important issue in Germany.

Contrary to the conventional wisdom, German pension liabilities are understated because, by law, companies base their calculations on facts as of the balance sheet date. No estimates of future salary increases or other factors affect the liability. As such, German pension liabilities resemble the accumulated benefit, not the projected benefit, which is the basis for pension accounting under U.S. GAAP and international standards.

■ *Japan.* Many people believe that Japanese earnings are understated by accounting differences, which would explain the high multiples. I do not accept this view. If anything, Japanese earnings are overstated, not understated. The biggest accounting differences in Japan apply to deferred taxes and pensions. Because of book–tax conformity, the normal situation in Japan is for taxable income to exceed book income, which results in potential deferred tax assets. These assets generally pertain to provisions and write-downs not allowable for tax purposes. Deferred taxes are generally not provided by Japanese companies (they are prohibited in the parent company financial statements and are optional in consolidation), which results in an understatement of reported results.

Japanese pensions consist of an unfunded severance liability and a funded defined-benefit pension plan. The funded plan is the largest element of pension cost at most companies. Because of unrealistic interest rate and earnings assumptions, Japanese pension plans are significantly underfunded. We estimate that the underfunding currently averages about 40 percent and is growing rapidly. The funded portion of the plan is accounted for on a cash basis with no recognition in the financial statements of the shortfall in funding. Under both U.S. GAAP and international standards, pension accounting is independent from the amount of funding, which increases the annual amount charged to expense and results in a liability in the balance sheet. This pension accounting deficit tends to offset the unrecognized deferred tax asset.

Japan will be adopting several accounting changes in fiscal 1999 and 2000, at which time the deferred tax and pension differences will disappear and Japanese financial reporting will be much closer to international standards than it is at the present time.

In explaining Japanese earnings, many people focus on the use of accelerated depreciation. Again, because of book–tax conformity, companies use tax-based accelerated depreciation for book purposes. The argument is that accelerated depreciation produces larger amounts of depreciation than the straight-line method, depressing Japanese earnings. This view is true only so long as the rate of investment is increasing, which is not the case in Japan. Furthermore, Japanese foreign subsidiaries do not have to conform their accounting to the Japanese parent, and most follow accounting practices mandated by their respective countries. As Japanese investment moves offshore, the use of Japanese tax-based accelerated depreciation is falling. As a result of the combination of a decrease in the rate of investment and increased offshore investment, depreciation charges reported by the majority of Japanese companies are lower than amounts that would be reported on a straight-line basis. Depreciation is overstating, not understating, earnings for the majority of Japanese companies.

Approaches to Valuation

Many valuation approaches are used, including P/E; enterprise value to earnings before interest, taxes, depreciation, and amortization (EV/EBITDA); price to sales; price to book; price to cash flow; and economic value added (EVA).

P/E. Earnings are the best valuation measure because of their inclusiveness. Accounting differences affect earnings, however, which obviates their use for cross-border comparative purposes unless adjustments are made. Fortunately, accounting differences do not affect every industry in the same way.

The average reported and comparative U.S. GAAP results differ by sector, as shown in **Table 8**. The smallest average adjustments are for chemicals, paper, steel, and airlines; the largest average adjustments are for automobiles and drugs. Unfortunately, the numbers for the airline and technology sectors may be misleading because these sectors have large swings in both directions. For life insurance, the differences are so extreme that investors should not use published financial information to make any comparison.

EV/EBITDA. Another approach to making comparisons on a cross-border basis is EV/EBITDA. This introduces a new basis of valuation that is based essentially on cash operating expense. One of the biggest problems with EBITDA is the omission of costs associated with a company's productive capacity. This omission is ludicrous for such capital-intensive industries as the auto industry, in which a

Table 8. U.S. GAAP Adjustments: Major Sector Differences

Category	Auto	Chemical	Food	Drug	Paper	Steel	Airlines	Technology	Life Insurance
Provisions	✔								
Goodwill/intangibles	✔		✔	✔		✔		✔	
Pensions	✔	✔				✔		✔	
Foreign exchange/ financial instruments	✔					✔	✔		
Deferred tax	✔				✔		✔	✔	
Depreciation	✔							✔	
Average adjustment	22%	4%	–10%	–24%	–6%	2%	3%[a]	–11%[a]	na

na = not applicable, because it is not possible to make adjustments based on published financial statements.

Note: Airlines average increase for six companies was 25 percent; average decrease for four companies was 34 percent. Technology average decrease for five companies was 46 percent; average increase for five companies was 24.3 percent.

[a]Significant increases and decreases offset.

---

major issue is how to deal with industry excess capacity. This approach also ignores differences in tax rates, which makes German and Japanese companies appear relatively more profitable on an EBITDA basis than they really are.

Price to Sales. The price-to-sales ratio is not suitable for use on a cross-border basis because differences too often reflect the underlying nature of the companies rather than relative valuation. Non-U.S. companies tend to be more diversified than U.S. companies, which affects this valuation criterion.

Price to Book. Book value is the worst basis for cross-border comparison. Book value is nothing more than a residual number—the difference between the assets and the liabilities that accounting recognizes. When the accounting rules change, the assets or liabilities change and the book value changes. For example, SFAS 106, Accounting for Postretirement Benefits Other Than Pension, reduced the book value of U.S. automobile companies by more than 50 percent when adopted. Although nothing of substance changed, book values definitely changed.

Price to Cash Flow. Cash is fine, but nobody uses cash. Analysts use a surrogate, such as income plus depreciation. Real cash is the most volatile and unpredictable number imaginable. Once analysts use a surrogate, they are simply using another number, such as income, and treating it like cash.

EVA. EVA has two problems: (1) computing the cost of capital, particularly in the current environment, and (2) deciding what to do with the many companies that do not have positive EVA.

Conclusion

Cross-border financial statement analysis can be very difficult because of the many accounting differences that exist among countries. Without making appropriate adjustments, such important valuation criteria as earnings, P/E, and price to book value may lack comparability when viewed in a global context. Although the differences are shrinking, clearly more harmonization will be required as global capital markets develop.

Question and Answer Session
Gary S. Schieneman

Question: Does any evidence exist that investors in Europe are doing cross-border comparisons?

Schieneman: Yes. Although the level of sophistication varies, European investors are more sophisticated about this subject than U.S. investors are because they invest on a cross-border basis more often than U.S. investors do.

Question: Can you expand on your comments about amortizing versus capitalizing goodwill and discuss the issue of penalizing organic growth versus growth through acquisition?

Schieneman: When a company makes an acquisition in a service or high-tech industry, the company is primarily acquiring an intangible asset. If the acquirer capitalizes and amortizes the intangible asset, it is associating a cost of acquiring these future earnings as they occur. Amortization of goodwill implies that only incremental earnings from an acquisition are part of postacquisition profit. That is, any earnings that the company reports are over and above what the acquirer paid. Had the company generated the same additional profits from organic growth, the cost of generating these increased profits would have been charged against income. Direct write-off of goodwill or capitalization with no amortization results in higher post-acquisition profits than would be the case under organic growth.

Question: Are there major differences between U.S. GAAP and the non-U.S. banking sector?

Schieneman: I have not approached the banking sector because doing so requires understanding local regulatory requirements. Each country has its own approach to regulating the financial services industry. Perhaps the most significant difference is how governments prescribe the criteria for the provisioning of bad loans.

Old and New Perspectives on Equity Risk

Philip S. Fortuna
Managing Director
Quantitative Group
Scudder Kemper Investments

> Standard deviation has been the risk metric of choice since the advent of modern portfolio theory in the 1950s. Its popularity, however, has more to do with convenience than effectiveness, and according to the criteria of measurement theory, standard deviation is not a valid risk-measurement tool. In contrast, downside risk not only has the advantage of both reliability and validity as a risk measure but advances in computer technology have made it easy to use as well.

Almost everyone would agree that accurate assessment of risk is critical for successful investment decision making. Despite all the work published on this issue, however, insufficient attention has been paid to appropriately measuring, defining, and assessing investment risk. As a result, the overwhelming majority of theoreticians, practitioners, and evaluators are using misspecified measures of investment risk, which has important implications for money managers and their clients.

This presentation begins with a brief history of investment risk, going back to first principles. Next, I address some new criteria for thinking about risk, evaluate several proposed risk measures based on those criteria, and try to explain whether the type of risk measure used makes a difference. The final piece of the puzzle is applying these findings in a fund management setting.

History of Investment Risk

Most investment professionals have seen, if not produced, reports that show the traditional risk–return scatterplot, in which risk is defined as the standard deviation of return. The typical reason for using standard deviation is, in effect, custom: Standard deviation is what people learned to use, the method they use at their company, or simply the "right" way. When asked, practitioners really have no idea *why* it is an industry standard. So, an interesting starting point is how standard deviation became the accepted way of measuring risk.

Harry Markowitz won a Nobel Prize for the work he did in the 1950s on portfolio selection. In his classic monograph *Portfolio Selection*, Markowitz laid out for academic economists how one should measure risk and construct portfolios. He suggested four criteria for choosing a risk measure: cost of calculation, convenience, familiarity, and quality of portfolios produced. Keep in mind that these criteria came from the perspective of someone in the 1950s who did not have access to today's cheap computing power.

Markowitz looked at a couple of definitions of risk and concluded that variance was the best risk measure to use because, compared with other measures, it was cheaper (i.e., used less computer time), more convenient (i.e., the application of the formula was straightforward), and familiar to other financial economists. Other measures, however, produced *better* portfolios. Only under one condition were variance-based portfolios as good as (not better than) those produced using another measure. We will return to this condition later.

For Markowitz, using variance was a convenient and simplifying assumption. Forty years have now passed since Markowitz came to his conclusions about the cost, convenience, and familiarity of using variance. The computing world has changed in a myriad of ways. Today, the average personal computer has more computing power than was available to the United States at the time of World War II. Therefore, one has to wonder whether standard deviation is still the most appropriate risk measure.

Measurement Theory

Measurement theory, a discipline that has been around longer than financial theory, may help answer the question of standard deviation's appropriateness. This discipline uses a number of criteria for evaluating the appropriateness of a measurement method. Three criteria in particular are relevant to the risk question:

- *Validity.* The concept of content validity deals with the extent to which a measure thoroughly and appropriately assesses the characteristics it is intended to measure.
- *Reliability.* The reliability criterion addresses the extent to which a measure is free from measurement error. Roughly speaking, a risk measure is considered reliable if the correlation is high between separate measurements at close points in time.
- *Utility.* The utility criterion addresses the usefulness of the measure. In the context of a risk measure, the utility criterion looks at whether the measure can be easily calculated, can serve as the basis for building useful portfolios, can be used to evaluate portfolio performance, and (least importantly) can be used to construct elegant theoretical models.

These quite logical criteria suggest that researchers should be looking for a measure of investment risk that measures what people actually think of as risk (validity), that gives roughly the same measurement over time (reliability), and that people can actually use (utility). The rest of this presentation uses these three criteria to compare the familiar standard deviation measure with other measures—specifically, the lower-partial-moment family of measures.

A simple way to think of lower-partial-moment measures of risk—a fairly abstract statistical concept—is that they judge risk relative to one's risk threshold, or the level below which one starts to feel pain. Suppose, for instance, a patient needs $100,000 for a liver transplant and will not get the liver transplant without the $100,000. So, $100,000 is the patient's threshold, not $105,000 or $110,000. Likewise, investors who need to maintain the principal of their investments will feel pain if they lose money. They will not feel pain if the S&P 500 Index has gone up 22 percent and their investments are up only 21 percent.

Notice that the risk threshold can vary from investor to investor, which makes it a very powerful concept. Given this concept of a risk threshold, three potentially useful risk measures exist that focus on only the following parts of the return distribution:

- *Downside frequency.* Downside frequency measures how often an investment is likely to fall below an investor's pain threshold. A downside frequency of 5 percent indicates that the investment will fall below the threshold 5 percent of the time. Downside frequency can be defined relative to whatever time horizon is appropriate for the investor.
- *Average downside.* Average downside measures the average shortfall in those periods when returns fell below the threshold.
- *Semivariance.* Semivariance, or the variance on the downside only, is actually a combination of downside frequency and average downside. Investors intuitively feel more risk if they have a higher probability of not meeting their goals and if, when they actually do miss their goals, they miss them by a lot rather than by a little bit. Semivariance for downside risk is defined relative to the investor's pain threshold, which is not necessarily zero. For an individual investor, the downside may be zero. For a pension plan, the downside may be calculated relative to an actuarial assumed growth rate.

Evaluating Validity

One way of thinking about the validity of a measure of investment risk is how well the measure correlates with investors' perceptions of investment risk. The measure should reflect the way investors think about risk and the way they actually behave rather than what researchers say investors *should* think about risk and how investors *should* behave.

Insights from Psychology. Research in the field of psychology shows that people simply do not perceive risk in terms of standard deviation. Payne (1973) analyzed how participants assessed risks associated with a set of gambles. For each gamble, he kept the expected payoff the same but changed various elements of risk. Some gambles had higher standard deviations than others, some had higher probability of losses, and others had higher potential losses. He found that standard deviation accounted for less than 2 percent of people's assessment of risk and that more-relevant criteria were probability of a loss (downside frequency) and the size of the possible loss (related to average downside). Such findings are common in the psychological literature.

Insights from Investment Management. Olsen (1997) surveyed 630 institutional portfolio managers and found that 47 percent of portfolio managers surveyed defined risk as a large loss or return below the target—in other words, downside risk. Looked at another way, if standard deviation is the ultimate measure of risk, then all those portfolio managers should have said they view unexpectedly high returns as risk, because high volatility is associated with exceptionally high as well as exceptionally low returns. Unfortunately, not one manager associated risk with unexpectedly high returns. Thus, variance cannot be a measure of portfolio managers judgment of risk.

After further analysis, Olsen found that portfolio managers identified four relevant risk attributes: the potential for large loss, the potential for below-target returns, the ability to control loss, and knowledge of the investment. The common denominator among these attributes is downside risk.

Insights from the Public. In a survey of 637 mutual fund buyers, the Investment Company Institute (1996) found that 51 percent said that they think of risk as the chance of losing money, 26 percent said risk was return versus chance of losing money, and 8 percent said risk was a failure to meet a target. So, 85 percent of mutual fund investors think about risk in a downside context. Only 6 percent said risk was volatility, but the word "volatility" was not used in the survey; "swings in the movement of your investment" was the way it was described to participants. Interestingly, a large plurality of mutual fund buyers said their target goal was zero. They simply did not want to lose money.

Summary. Data from psychological research, investment managers, and the public indicate that standard deviation does *not* correlate with people's perception of risk. Downside risk is more salient in people's minds than volatility. In other words, people feel pain when returns fall below their risk threshold. This fact should be incontrovertible at this point, but it is not. Many people in investment management do not seem to care what the public actually thinks of as risk, and these same people hold fast to the belief that standard deviation does a good job of capturing investment risk.

Evaluating Reliability

Reliability focuses on whether risk is measured consistently from period to period. The argument given by some people for why they use standard deviation is that, although semivariance is a good idea, it is very unstable. They argue that semivariance is changing all the time because only the downside observations are used. So, in a three-year up market, only 10 downside months might exist. Thus, semivariance is inherently unstable, they claim, because it uses only a portion of the 36 months of data. Standard deviation, in contrast, is supposedly much more stable because all the data are used.

At Scudder Kemper Investments, we looked at actual mutual fund returns through time for two bond categories (GNMA and Income) and two equity categories (Large Blend and Mid Growth) in order to evaluate in practice the reliability of standard deviation and the lower-partial-moment measures. We used funds that had at least $100 million in assets as of December 31, 1996. Although the results do not change with a smaller asset cutoff, we did not want the results to be biased by the idiosyncrasies that can occur with small funds. We looked at rolling three-year returns over the period from January 1991 to December 1996 and ranked the funds on various risk measures. To remove the impact of different market levels over time, we analyzed risk rankings rather than the absolute levels of risk.

We ranked the funds in each group on each measure every month on a rolling-three-year basis. We looked at the correlations between where a fund ranked in terms of risk at certain intervals—1 month, 3 months, and 12 months forward—to see how stable the rankings were through time. If standard deviation is considered to be stable, then risk rankings based on standard deviation should have very high correlations over time.[1] **Table 1** shows the average correlations for large growth funds (and results were similar for the other groups). For the one-month-forward comparison, all of the correlations are very high for all measures. Moving forward 12 months, however, the correlation of rankings for the three-year standard deviation measure dropped to 0.80.

Table 1. Average Correlations between Three-Year Risk Measures for Large Growth Funds over Different Rolling Time Periods

Measure	1 Month	3 Months	12 Months
Standard deviation	0.98	0.95	0.80
Downside frequency	0.97	0.91	0.69
Average downside	0.98	0.93	0.76
Semivariance	0.98	0.95	0.79
Return	0.97	0.90	0.65

As predicted by downside-risk bashers, the correlation of the rankings for three-year downside frequency drops further to 0.69. Thus, over one year, downside frequency is relatively unstable compared with standard deviation—a correlation of 0.69 versus 0.80. Because the reliability criterion suggests that we

---

[1]Note that even 12 months later, 24 data points are unchanged in a rolling three-year calculation, and thus we expect high correlations. We could use corrections for this dependence, but in this case, a relative comparison of correlations is adequate.

need consistency in measurement over similar measurement periods, the only conclusion is that downside frequency is not very reliable.

The three-year average-downside measure also shows a diminishing pattern of correlations over time, but it is actually not much more unstable than standard deviation (0.76 versus 0.80 for the 12-month comparison).

Most importantly, the three-year semivariance measure, which is the standard deviation on the downside, has essentially the same reliability as the standard deviation measure (0.79 versus 0.80). In other words, downside risk as measured by downside volatility is as stable as using standard deviation. Thus, the argument that the inclusion of fewer data points makes semivariance less reliable does not hold water in practice.

As a comparison, look at three-year return correlations. One month forward, it is 0.97; twelve months forward, 0.65. This slippage exists even with two years of data in common. One can see why past performance is not necessarily an indicator of future performance. Risk (as would be expected) is actually more stable than return (a 12-month correlation of 0.79 versus 0.65).

Evaluating Utility

Research shows that people do not think of risk as standard deviation; they think of it in a downside context. Thus, standard deviation fails the *validity* criterion, but all of the downside-risk measures pass. In addition, semivariance is as consistent as standard deviation. That is, semivariance is as *reliable* as standard deviation.

The final question is whether the type of risk measure used makes a difference. The utility criterion relates to whether the risk measure is useful—that is, can it be used to build better portfolios and evaluate portfolio performance?

In theory, variance and semivariance measures produce the same results if one key condition holds: Returns must be normally distributed.[2] Recent academic research suggests that many return distributions are nonnormal, but there is a more visually interesting way to determine whether returns are normally distributed. We looked at every Scudder bond fund that had a five-year record over the period ending December 1996. **Figure 1** shows a plot of the return distribution for one of these funds: the Scudder Global Bond Fund. The distribution of this fund (and indeed of all of the other Scudder funds examined) is obviously not normal.

Figure 1. Monthly Return Distribution for Scudder Global Bond Fund, April 1991–December 1996

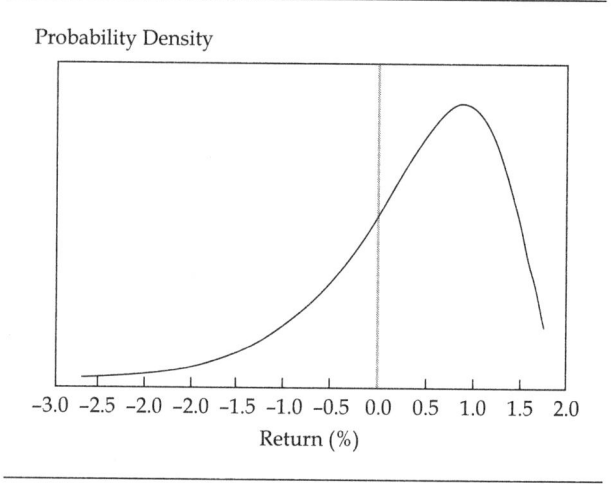

Clearly, the theoretical conditions under which variance and semivariance produce identical results are not found in the real world. The question, however, remains: Does the choice of risk measure make a practical difference? Our work shows that it can. **Figure 2** shows the performance of the Scudder Development Fund relative to all of its peers on a rolling-three-year basis (ending September 1997). In terms of standard deviation, this fund, which is in the third quartile in terms of risk, has been more risky than average, but the level of risk has been fairly stable. On a downside-risk basis, this fund actually had a tremendous increase in downside risk, bringing it near the 90th percentile in terms of downside risk. To produce such downside risk, this fund had big losses relative to its risk threshold—in this case, relative to zero. So, despite its losses, the fund managed to have fairly stable standard deviations by having big losses and small gains.

Figure 3 shows another Scudder product, the Growth and Income Fund, that appears to have a fairly stable standard deviation. In terms of downside risk, however, it deteriorated from 1994 until mid-1996, when it dropped into the second quartile, but then improved quite a bit. We lost assets during this period. Management noticed the problem, corrected it, and the fund again became an asset gainer.

---

[2]Actually, variance and semivariance measures produce the same results only if returns are symmetric in a special way, and normality is the most frequently used assumption that meets this condition.

Figure 2. Rolling Risk and Return of Scudder Development Fund, September 1990–September 1997

Note: Shaded lines indicate quartile rankings.

Figure 3. Rolling Risk and Return of Scudder Growth and Income Fund, September 1990–September 1997

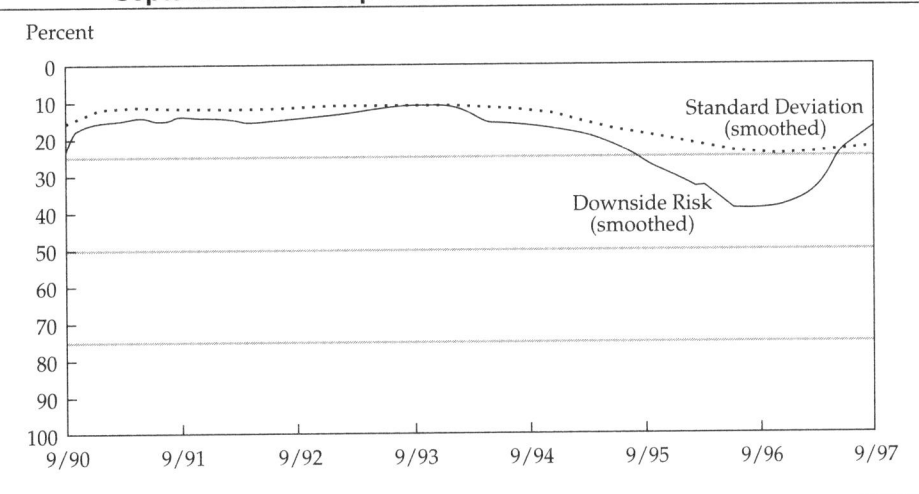

Note: Shaded lines indicate quartile rankings.

Asset Allocation Test

An interesting test of a risk measure is how well it performs in asset allocation. Some people have argued that downside risk does not work in certain types of markets. For example, Kaplan and Siegel (1994) consider Japan in the 1980s and 1990s. They assert that a manager using downside risk in Japan during the 1980s would have been fully invested in Japan as the market skyrocketed because there was no downside risk. In the early 1990s, however, the market crashed.

To investigate this criticism, we decided to test how well downside risk would have worked as part of an asset allocation process between Japanese and U.S. equities from January 1970 to December 1996. This period provides a good test because it includes the rise and fall of the Japanese equity market and the rise, fall, and rise of the U.S. equity market.

To avoid controversy over forecasting methods, we based the return forecast on rolling past-10-year returns. We calculated two efficient frontiers using standard software: a mean–variance optimizer and a downside-risk optimizer. For mean–variance optimization, we decided to solve the infinite-number-of-solutions problem by simply maximizing the Sharpe ratio. For downside risk, we maximized the Sortino ratio, which is the ratio of return to downside risk. We used a 10 percent risk-threshold point because, at the time we did the study, the long-term return on

U.S. equities was 10 percent and we reasoned that U.S. investors would not invest in Japanese equities if they could not earn more than 10 percent (like most U.S. mutual fund investors, we ignored diversification as a reason for investing in Japanese equities). We reestimated variables quarterly and assumed zero transaction costs.[3]

Table 2 shows the results for portfolios constructed using mean–variance optimization and downside-risk optimization, as well as one with a neutral 50/50 split (U.S. equities/Japanese equities), one containing 100 percent U.S. equities, and one containing 100 percent Japanese equities. The annualized return for a portfolio invested only in U.S. equities during the 1980–96 period was 16.2 percent, versus 13.7 percent for Japan only; the 50/50 split portfolio had a return between the two (15.8 percent). With mean–variance optimization, the annualized return improved significantly (17.3 percent), and although the standard deviation was a little higher than that of the 50/50 portfolio (18.3 percent versus 17.3 percent), it had a higher Sharpe ratio (0.52 versus 0.47). Unfortunately, even though the return of the mean–variance portfolio was higher than that of the 100 percent U.S. portfolio, its Sharpe ratio was a little lower (0.52 versus 0.59). So, from a return standpoint, mean–variance optimization worked quite well.

The downside-risk characteristics of a mean–variance portfolio, however, were actually much worse than for the U.S.-only portfolio and even worse than for the Japanese-only portfolio, meaning the mean–variance portfolio would have had more quarters in which it missed the threshold (or had larger shortfalls) than a portfolio invested in either U.S. or Japanese equities alone. It also would have had some very good quarters, because the standard deviation of the mean–variance portfolio was fairly high compared with the U.S.-only portfolio but still not as high as the Japanese-only portfolio. As a result, the mean–variance portfolio's Sortino ratio was poor relative to the U.S.-only portfolio (0.39 versus 0.78) but better than the 50/50 portfolio (0.39 versus 0.24).

The downside-risk-optimized portfolio had the highest annualized return, 20.0 percent, of all the portfolios. Its standard deviation was roughly 3 percentage points higher than that of the mean–variance portfolio (21.6 percent versus 18.3 percent), but its downside risk was much lower (11.3 percent versus 18.8 percent). The realized Sharpe ratio was actually higher for the downside-risk portfolio than for the mean–variance portfolio (0.57 versus 0.52—remember that for the mean–variance optimization, we were attempting to maximize the Sharpe ratio), and the Sortino ratio for the downside-risk portfolio (0.89) was the highest of any of the allocation rules.

Although I would hardly suggest allocating assets using such a naive forecasting rule, the findings of this study clearly demonstrate that the risk measure used *can* make a difference.

Application of Findings

Using these findings, we have created a performance measurement approach that we use internally to evaluate our managers. Because we believe that risk measures should capture people's actual attitudes and behavior toward risk and return, our focus is on total return, with risk measured as downside risk with a zero target. We use rolling returns and peer universes that correspond to widely recognized standards, such as a Lipper or Morningstar category.

We have a very simple goal: We want to have a lot of funds and products up in the northwest quadrant of risk–return space (i.e., low risk and high return). At this stage, we do not try to figure out why the product performed as it did, but we simply try to show how successful we are overall relative to the competition and how successful each product is at meeting its risk–return goals.

---

[3] In other studies, we included transaction costs, but the results did not substantially change.

Table 2. Characteristics of Simulated Portfolios Containing Japanese and U.S. Equities, January 1980–December 1996

Characteristic	Mean–Variance Optimization	Downside-Risk Optimization	50/50[a]	U.S. Only	Japanese Only
Annualized return	17.3%	20.0%	15.8%	16.2%	13.7%
Standard deviation	18.3%	21.6%	17.3%	14.5%	26.4%
Downside risk	18.8%	11.3%	24.3%	8.1%	15.8%
Sharpe ratio	0.52	0.57	0.47	0.59	0.23
Sortino ratio	0.39	0.89	0.24	0.78	0.24

[a]50 percent U.S. equities and 50 percent Japanese equities.

Figure 4. Three-Year Rolling Return, Downside Risk, and Sortino Ratio Percentile Rankings for Scudder Growth and Income Fund, April 1988–March 1998

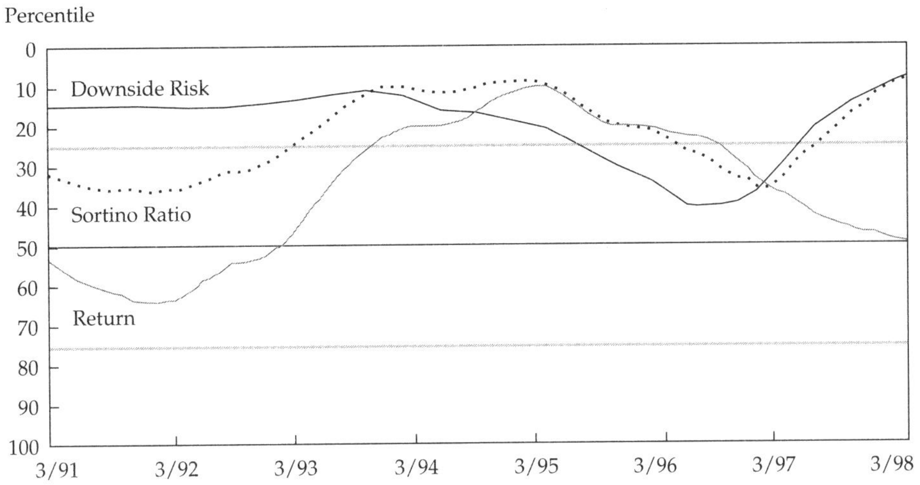

Note: Shaded lines indicate quartile rankings; solid quartile line represents the median. Ranking data for 296 funds in the Morningstar Large Blend peer universe. Data smoothed by taking 12-month moving average.

Based on three-year rolling percentile rankings, as shown **Figure 4**, the Scudder Growth and Income Fund was a third-quartile fund on a total return basis through the early 1990s and then moved into the first and second quartile relative to peers. Notice that its downside risk was always first or second quartile, and as a result, its risk-adjusted return, which is the Sortino ratio, was either first or second quartile.

This same analysis can be done on a fund-family level. **Figure 5** plots the ranking (relative to the peer universe) of each fund in our fund family on downside-risk percentiles and on return percentiles for the three-year period ending in December 1997. Out of 25 of our funds, 13 are in the northwest quadrant (low risk, high return). An interesting aspect of Figure 5 is that, on balance, the *lower* the downside risk, the *higher* the monthly return. (If we had looked at these funds in terms of absolute returns and absolute risks rather than relative to their peers, we would have seen a quite different kind of relationship.) In the downside-risk world over this time period, the correlations between risk and return were often close to zero, which has enormous implications. If these conditions are sustained over time, investors can have superior return performance and low downside risk, but the price is higher total volatility. Thus, the practical potential for using downside risk is tremendous.

Conclusion

Although standard deviation is reliable, it is not valid in the technical sense of measurement theory. Downside risk is valid and reliable and, with modern computers, easy to calculate. The choice of the risk measure can make a big difference in the realized return. So, the question is not why define risk as downside risk but rather, why not?

Markowitz wrote:

> The proper procedure, it seems to me, is to start with analyses based on variance. Analyses based on semivariance . . . can be considered after experience is gained with simpler measures. In the choice of criteria, as well as in other respects, the form of analysis must be expected to evolve. (p. 194)

Investment managers have now had 40 years of experience with volatility; it is time for their risk analysis to evolve.

Figure 5. Three-Year Risk–Return Percentile Ranking for Scudder, Kemper, and AARP Investment Program Equity Funds, December 31, 1994, through December 31, 1997

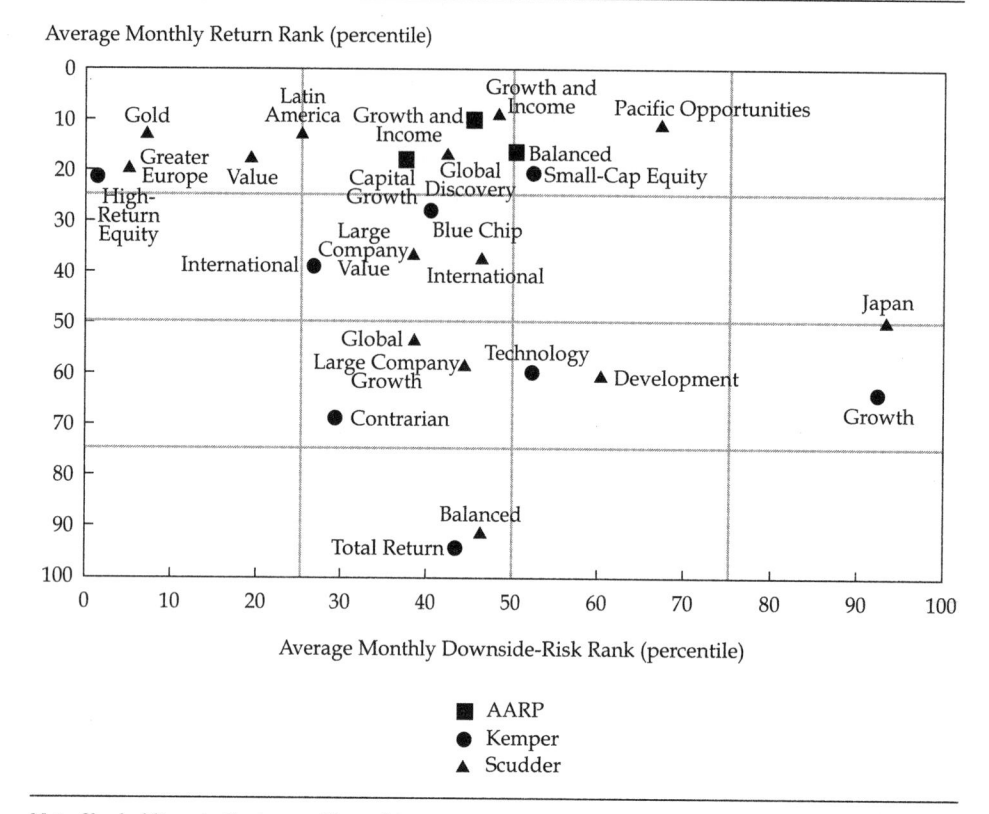

Note: Shaded lines indicate quartile rankings.

Question and Answer Session
Philip S. Fortuna

Question: How do you recommend measuring an investor's risk threshold, and how do you incorporate this threshold in investor profiling?

Fortuna: If you are running a mutual fund family, the safest course of action is probably to assume a zero threshold because that is what the research shows is true for a strong plurality of clients. Mutual funds deal with a huge number of clients, so you can't really tailor a fund to each client. We have structured some asset-allocation-based products for which we do downside-risk optimizations based on individual clients' risk thresholds. We actually surveyed these clients to approximate the risk threshold for an individual. You can determine this threshold the same way that you do utility measurements: Give people choices, see what kind of choices they make, and infer their risk thresholds.

The most difficult problem, which is endemic, is that risk preferences are nonstationary. When we surveyed some clients in May 1998, we got one set of risk thresholds. People said they had long-term horizons, they were willing to wait five years, and so on. We resurveyed some of the same people at the end of August 1998, and their risk preferences had shifted to the short end—their investment horizons were 1–3 years instead of 5–10 years. Their actual tolerance for losses had suddenly disappeared. A large portion of the difference was changing reference points. So, they were not thinking that their total gain had been X and that they were still way ahead. They were thinking that they were down 20 percent from the peak, not that they were up 80 percent from when they made this investment. Thus, shifting risk thresholds make the analysis very difficult.

Question: What tools are available from vendors for downside-risk optimization?

Fortuna: Some of the vendors who have implemented downside risk have got it wrong. Here is what to look out for. If I were to tell you that my monthly standard deviation was X, what would you tell me is my annual standard deviation, based only on knowing that information? The standard answer is to multiply the monthly value by the square root of 12. A lot of people have implemented downside risk, calculated downside risk on a monthly basis, and multiplied it by the square root of 12, which is absolutely wrong. Any math department will tell you that you can't take a lower partial moment and multiply it by the square root of 12. The math doesn't work. So, a vendor calculating annual downside risk by multiplying the monthly value by the square root of 12 will get the wrong result.

Some people are doing it right. Frank Sortino, who is with the Pension Research Institute in San Francisco, and Brian Rom, who is with Sponsor Software in New York, are two leaders in the field who are working on developing software for practitioners. They're both aware of the problems, and they have good mathematical techniques for dealing with them.

The Value Added by Equity Analysts

Kent L. Womack
Associate Professor of Finance
Tuck School of Business Administration at Dartmouth College

> Because many investors depend on sell-side equity analysts' forecasts and recommendations, the reliability of this information is critical to the investment decision-making process. Although research shows that sell-side analysts can add value in some areas, research also indicates that the accuracy of some information is suspect and that analysts' decisions may be compromised by behavioral biases. Investors can take advantage of the fact that some analyst biases may be predictable and can use this knowledge to distinguish between credible and dubious analysis.

The information provided by sell-side equity analysts is a major input in making equity investment management decisions. Thus, investors must decide to what extent they should rely on the evaluations made by these analysts. This decision depends on the answers to two questions: First, is the ultimate goal of sell-side equity analysts identifying undervalued investments (or to what extent are their decisions influenced by factors other than strict analysis)? Second, how good are these analysts at predicting future earnings and share prices?

Simply knowing that analysts identify undervalued stocks somewhat more than half the time would not be very interesting or useful. If investors knew, however, that analysts were *predictably* wrong at certain times and in certain directions—that is, that their errors were somewhat *systematic* because of various agency biases and behavioral foibles—then investors' potential ability to debias analysts' information and use it profitably would be enhanced.

This presentation focuses on a line of research I have been pursuing for about eight years: how equity analysts make decisions and whether they add value. Finding answers requires evaluating analysts' decision-making processes and assessing their task accuracy. Because of data availability, the research is based solely on the decisions of sell-side equity analysts. Until the advent of First Call and other research services, obtaining reasonably comprehensive and unbiased data on sell-side equity analysts was not easy (and obtaining comprehensive and unbiased buy-side data is, for now, not feasible).

Equity analysts perform three main tasks—forecasting earnings, recommending the best stocks (within the followed universe), and assisting in the sale of new issues of securities to investors. In analyzing these tasks, the first area of concern is determining what analysts are trying to do. Is their ultimate goal to predict today's undervalued securities and to estimate future returns on stocks in their universe?

The next challenge is to assess the task accuracy of sell-side analysts. In other words, how well do analysts perform their functions? Specifically, the analysis focuses on the accuracy of analysts' earnings forecasts and their securities recommendations.

One general conclusion is that the work of security analysts is, in fact, valuable but that this value is conditional; it is valuable in some circumstances but not in others. Information from analysts, therefore, should be viewed critically.

Forecasting Earnings

Forecasting earnings per share is the first task of analysts. Tracking earnings forecasting is a huge subindustry in the investment business. The growth of I/B/E/S International, First Call, and others that compile earnings forecasts and the fact that a separate ranking category exists on the *Institutional Investor* All-America Research Team for analysts with the highest earnings accuracy show the importance of such accuracy. Earnings are highly correlated with stock prices, so identifying the most accurate earn-

---

Professor Womack's World Wide Web page is mba.tuck.dartmouth.edu/pages/faculty/kent.womack.

ings estimates most of the time is tantamount to "minting" impressive investment returns.

Unfortunately, evidence suggests that analysts are less than impressive at accurately forecasting earnings. For example, Dreman and Berry (1995a) evaluated the accuracy of analysts' earnings estimates. They examined consensus analyst forecasts from 1974 through the first quarter of 1991. They found that analysts are off by more than 10 percent more than 55 percent of the time, that analyst errors are increasing over time, and that analysts are optimistic on average. The authors concluded that behavioral factors may play an important role for analysts in forecasting earnings.

So, one interpretation of the evidence suggests that analysts' ability to forecast earnings is somewhere between mediocre and bad. Interestingly, the current level of forecasting accuracy exists *despite the fact* that analysts and companies communicate regularly. Companies have a genuine incentive to contribute to the accuracy of analysts' estimates to avoid any dislocation in their stock price caused by a surprise on the earnings reporting day. Even so, substantial earnings surprises do occur.

This point raises serious questions: Why do analysts not make better earnings forecasts? Is the task too difficult because earnings are volatile, or is something else happening? How much should analysts listen to companies? Are analysts listening too carefully or not carefully enough? One would think that analysts *should* be better off by listening to management than by not. In terms of investors' ability to process both company and analyst information and come to the right conclusions, the proposition is at least possible that investors may do better to process each strand of information (analysts' and management's) separately rather than to let analysts preprocess management's information for them.

One important piece of the puzzle has been provided by Chopra (1998), who found that analysts are indeed optimistic on average but that a substantial part of forecast errors are negatively correlated with business cycle changes. That is, analysts' errors reflect their failure to grasp the macroeconomic growth changes rather than company-specific issues.

Recommending Stocks

Choosing the most attractive stock investments for investors is another critical role that analysts take on. Most investment brokerage houses provide customers with a "buy list" or "recommended list" of attractive investments. Not surprisingly, many more of these recommendations are positive than negative. According to various researchers, the ratio of buy signals to sell signals by analysts during the early 1990s was at least 15 to 1. Today, this ratio may be even higher, given the agency conflicts that inevitably occur when analysts give unfavorable forecasts or recommendations of companies they follow.

Stock recommendations are one of the truest reflections of the skill and judgment of analysts. Investors should know that accurate prediction of future stock prices is extraordinarily difficult and represents the ultimate test of stock market skill. Academics have argued for decades that analysts' success at stock picking is more likely to be pure luck rather than skill. According to the efficient market hypothesis, the market impounds information immediately into stock prices, and thus the advocates of efficient markets would argue that recommendations should have no value to potential purchasers after dissemination of the news. According to Grossman and Stiglitz (1980), however, this view of efficiency is naive. Investors need analysts as information "snoopers" to keep markets efficient by finding over- and underpriced stocks. Grossman and Stiglitz theorize that analysts must receive some payment for their efforts. The likely payment is the profits that they and their customers make from their identification of mispriced stocks. That is, in equilibrium, analysts must have enough predictive power to enable them to make enough money to stay in business.

Effects of Recommendations on Valuation. Given the theoretical backdrop, a key question becomes, what effect do analysts have in their role as information snoopers? Do their pronouncements move stocks towards new valuation levels? If so, are these new levels obtained immediately, or are there opportunities to trade and profit because the market takes a while to digest the news and revalue the stocks? In my Ph.D. thesis, I examined buy and sell recommendations issued from 1989 through 1991, and others have replicated my research using more-recent data. This research focuses on the following question: Taking recommendations at face value—new buy recommendations, new sell recommendations, and removals from either buy or sell recommendations—how did the stocks fare before, at the time of, and after the recommendations or removals? The financial press, including the *Wall Street Journal*, regularly conducts such studies. Most of the time, however, the press focuses not on risk-adjusted returns but simply on raw returns.

I conducted my analysis of analyst recommendations using several risk-adjusted methodologies. I used three risk adjustments—market, size, and the Fama and French (1992) three-factor model—to incorporate aspects necessary to satisfy the academic critique "If only you had adjusted for risk properly, there would be no excess returns." In the final analysis, all three methodologies pointed to the same conclusions, which would tend to mitigate many risk-based counter-conclusions.

I also examined the issue of the relative predictive value of buy recommendations versus sell recommendations. In addition, I wanted to look into whether analysts are market or momentum timers or whether their prognostications are driven by industry or individual stock issues.

Womack (1996), the published academic paper based on my Ph.D. thesis, examined about 1,600 buy recommendations of the top 14 U.S. brokers and all the sell recommendations of the same brokers over the 1989–91 period. Remember that analysts make many more buy recommendations than sell recommendations—about 15 to 1. **Figure 1** illustrates the outcome of this event study. Zero on the horizontal axis represents the day when a new recommendation is released, with each number representing the time in months before or after the announcement. The vertical axis shows the price relative to the recommendation event date on a risk-adjusted basis. A value greater than 1.00 on the price axis indicates a positive *excess* return; a value less than 1.00 indicates a negative *excess* return. For example, when the buy recommendations line goes above 1.00, the stocks with buy recommendations have, on average, accumulated positive excess returns. When the sell recommendations line goes down for a few months after Time 0, the stocks with sell recommendations have, on average, underperformed the market because they have negative *excess* returns.

■ *Buy recommendations.* During the six months prior to the announcement of a buy recommendation, no excess return occurs. Thus, buy recommendations appear to reflect stock picking more than momentum chasing. On the day of the recommendation, these stocks go up, on average, about 2.50 percent, and then continue to increase for the next month by another 2.25–2.50 percent. Farther out, the line is flat. An implication of these findings is that after new buy recommendations, an investment opportunity occurs in the first 4–6 weeks.

In other words, in contrast to the efficient market hypothesis, excess returns persist beyond the announcement date. By buying the stocks on the day of or the day after the buy recommendations and holding them for a month or so, investors can earn,

Figure 1. Effect of Buy and Sell Recommendations on Stock Price, 1989–91

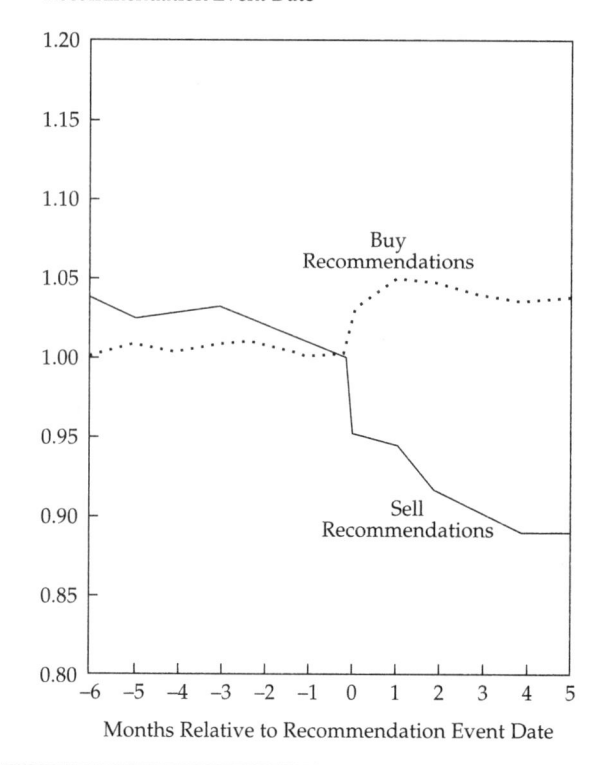

Source: Based on data from Womack (1996).

on average and ignoring transaction costs, more than a 2.25 percent excess return. Although the actual return for investors would depend on their transaction costs, this positive excess return is more than most academics would have anticipated for so short a period. To outperform the market by 2.25 percent in a month—on an annualized basis—represents a high return that is not explicable based simply on risk adjustments.

■ *Sell recommendations.* The sell recommendation data are more interesting than the buy recommendation data and reveal three important findings. First, stocks, on average, performed poorly in the months before the sell recommendations. Thus, typically, the market has already recognized that the company is doing poorly. Issuing a sell recommendation requires courage because many companies will deny further information to analysts who historically have made unfavorable pronouncements about their stocks.

Second, the announcement effect is approximately twice as large for sell recommendations as it is for buy recommendations. Although Figure 1 depicts only four months, a six-month examination of sell recommendations *after* the recommendation itself would show that the stocks continued to drift lower and underperformed the market by about 9 percent for the duration of this period.

The third conclusion, therefore, is that sell recommendations are a more powerful and more opportunistic trading signal of future price movements than are new buy recommendations. The excess returns to sell recommendations are larger *and* take the market longer to digest. Obviously, analysts do not issue as many sell signals, but when they do, their sell signals tend to be very powerful.

■ *Removals of buy recommendations.* Removals of buy recommendations occur almost as often as the placement of new buy recommendations. As **Figure 2** shows, the average stock that is pulled from a brokerage house's recommended list has outperformed the market by about 5 percent over the past two or three months before the removal. After analysts remove the buy recommendations, the stocks, on average, experience negative excess returns for the next 3 to 4 months. Total underperformance of stocks after a buy removal is about 7 percent. So, as investment signals, removals of buy recommendations are almost as powerful and tradeworthy as sell recommendations. The removals provide larger excess returns than new buy recommendations and move toward a new price level over a longer period of time.

Findings. So, the first result is that the positive (new buy) recommendations of these analysts are modestly valuable. Investors can gain a couple of percentage points of return, which is probably more (but not substantially more) than their trading costs. These returns, however, are very short lived. If investors wait a month or six weeks to use that new information, they cannot earn superior risk-adjusted returns. The statistical evidence shows that new buy recommendations are not predictively valuable five or six weeks after the recommendation. The negative information—new sell recommendations and removals of buy recommendations—seems not only to be correct but also to have predictive power for a longer period of time, up to six months. Stocks with negative information experience negative performance.

This conclusion naturally raises the question: If markets are efficient, why does the adjustment take so long? The difference may be found in behavioral issues explained by an idea called the endowment effect. Investors appear to believe the information more and be more opportunistic or open minded about stocks they do not own and can buy; they are less open minded about stocks they already own and of which they presumably already have a positive

Figure 2. Investment Value of Analysts' Removals of Buy Recommendations, 1989–91

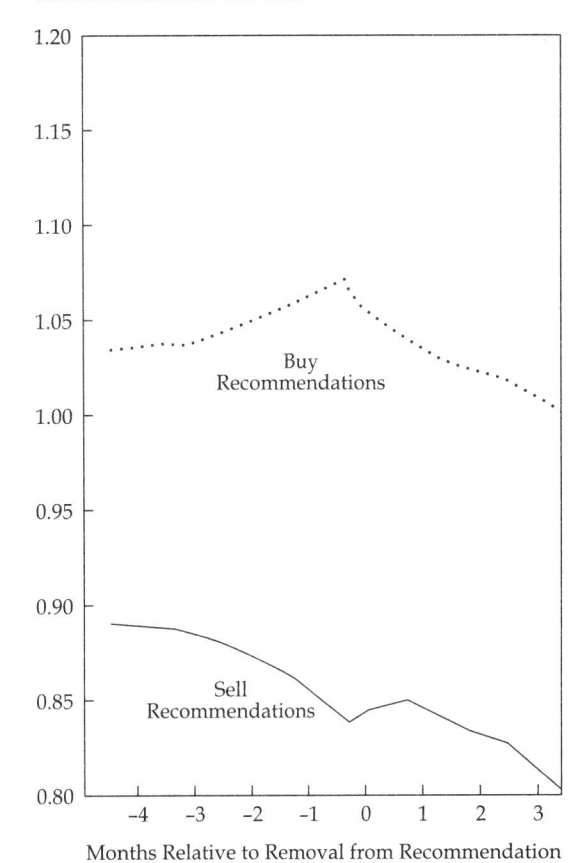

Source: Based on data from Womack (1996).

opinion. Whether or not this interpretation of the findings is correct, the market does not appear to impound the negative news as rapidly as the positive news.

This study uncovered several other interesting findings. When stocks are ranked by deciles (the 9th and 10th deciles represent large-cap stocks; lower deciles represent small-cap stocks), small-cap stocks respond (prices drift) much more vigorously than large-cap stocks do to new buy recommendations. The predictive power (excess return) after the first day is also much larger. In fact, it is about double for reasonably small-sized stocks in the 5th and 6th deciles relative to large-cap stocks in the 9th and 10th deciles. One might also ask whether the excess returns are the result of stock picking or market timing. In my judgment, the excess returns mostly reflect the former.

Interestingly, my analysis suggests that analysts focus on different fundamentals when making buy and sell recommendations. For buy recommendations, analysts are trying to pick a particular stock, not an industry, and thus are capturing mostly a stock-specific return. When analysts are announcing negative news and removing stocks from the recommended list, their recommendations tend to focus on the industry fundamentals because the industry returns are more negative than the stock returns.

In recommendations, one of the most important and most investment-oriented points is that a substantial asymmetry exists between the value of positive news, which is modest, and the value of negative news, which is quite valuable. When analysts make "sell" or "remove from buy" recommendations, investors should watch out.

A recent study by Barber, Lehavy, McNichols, and Trueman (1999) also examines whether investors can profitably use analysts' recommendations or, as the authors put it, "profit from the prophets." Although not done in an event-study context, this study is similar in other respects to my thesis paper on recommendations but uses a much larger sample. Moreover, the authors reach similar conclusions. They find that the value of buy recommendations is positive but reasonably small and that the predictive value of sell recommendations or negative downgrades of recommendations is robustly larger than for positive recommendations. They also find that the average consensus recommendation has value but not if investors wait 30 days to act on the revisions. The important finding of both studies is that the value of buy recommendations is gone within a month but the value of negative recommendations is larger and lasts longer.

The Reasons Given in Recommendations. Obviously, analysts may be better at some things than at others. An important challenge for investors, therefore, is to identify what cognitive tasks analysts can do well. Determining where an analyst's strengths lie is difficult because a single recommendation is composed of such a wide variety of analyses. One means through which it is possible to gain an insight into an analyst's strengths is to examine the reasoning that the analyst gives for his or her recommendations.

Although many reasons can be found in the texts written by analysts when they recommend a stock, two major categories regularly come into play. The first broad category for a buy recommendation is that a stock is cheap relative to its historical valuation. The second broad category is that the analyst believes something new is happening in the company, such as a cost-cutting initiative or a new product.

I conducted a pilot study for research now in progress using these two categories to determine which was the better predictor of future success in the company. Results indicate that over a period of three to six months, the answer is the "new initiative" category. Recommendations based on "attractive valuation" typically have little measurable value. Buy recommendations based on new information have much more predictive power than the average buy recommendation. Apparently, analysts cannot outpredict the consensus of the market about a stock's valuation. A stock that is cheap relative to historical norms is probably cheap for a reason. In other words, the market has impounded this information into stock prices. What analysts can do is predict the future events that the market has not completely impounded into stock prices.

Selling New Issues

A third task of analysts is assisting those in their brokerage firm in selling new issues of securities to investors. Underwriting transactions is highly profitable for both the firm and the analyst. Investors regularly report that brokerage salespeople spend a disproportionate amount of time selling new issues of securities rather than informing investors about news in seasoned securities. Interestingly, analysts are more involved in the underwriting process today than they were 15 or 20 years ago. Prior to and during the early 1980s, the analyst typically was not involved in analyzing new deals until after the "road show" was finished and the pricing was done.

Today, the analyst is the main "pitch person" in trying to sell new issues to investors. For such work, analysts are very well paid. For example, I recently spoke with an M.B.A. graduate who was an analyst following a high-tech industry that had many underwriting opportunities. He had been at one brokerage firm for two years when he was wooed away by another firm that doubled his salary to $600,000. In comparison, M.B.A.s in the corporate finance/underwriting areas of his firm were making, on average, about $250,000. This example supports the opinion that, in industries for which underwriting is a major part of revenues, underwriters engage in substantial competition for analysts.

Kringman, Shaw, and Womack (forthcoming 2000) surveyed chief financial officers to determine why their companies switched to a new lead underwriter for a second offering. We also analyzed other empirical data for switchers versus nonswitchers and, using probit regressions, tried to show what factors are key considerations when companies decide to switch underwriters and when they do not.

The top reasons to switch were to gain "research coverage"—especially the research coverage of an "influential analyst." Another reason was to "trade up" to an underwriter with a loftier reputation than the previous underwriter. Often, the main issue was whether the new underwriter's analyst was a member of the *Institutional Investor* All-America Research Team in the issuer's industry.

The Conflicts of Underwriting and the Credibility of Recommendations. Michaely and Womack (1999) explored the extent to which underwriting creates conflicts of interest. Users of analysts' information hope that analysts are trying to provide the best unbiased information that they have. On the other hand, analysts who are employed by an investment bank may have an ulterior motive: generating profits for their own firm by consummating extremely lucrative new issues.

The Michaely and Womack study examines the potential for conflicts in initial public offerings (IPOs) and seeks to determine how analysts choose between the potentially conflicting goals of preserving their long-term reputation ("truth telling") and generating profits for their companies ("rent seeking"). We compare recommendations by the underwriter analyst with recommendations by all other analysts during the first year after the IPO. The results show that the behavior of the underwriter analyst is quite suspicious.

Figure 3 compares buy recommendations by non-underwriters with buy recommendations by underwriters. Together, the three lines show how much the buy-and-hold cumulative returns change over the 12 months following the IPO. The immediate result is that investors discount the initial information in the underwriter's buy recommendation. Apparently, professional investment managers attempt to debias the recommendations of stocks that are offered by underwriters, or else these recommendations are more anticipated by the market. During the three-day event window around the recommendation, the stocks recommended by underwriters increased, on average, by 2.7 percent, compared with 4.4 percent for nonunderwriters. Over the 12-month period, the recommendations of the underwriters fared much worse than the recommendations of others.

Recommendations by analysts unaffiliated with the underwriter had remarkably good predictive

Figure 3. Performance Comparison for Companies Receiving New Buy Recommendations within One Year of IPO, 1990–91

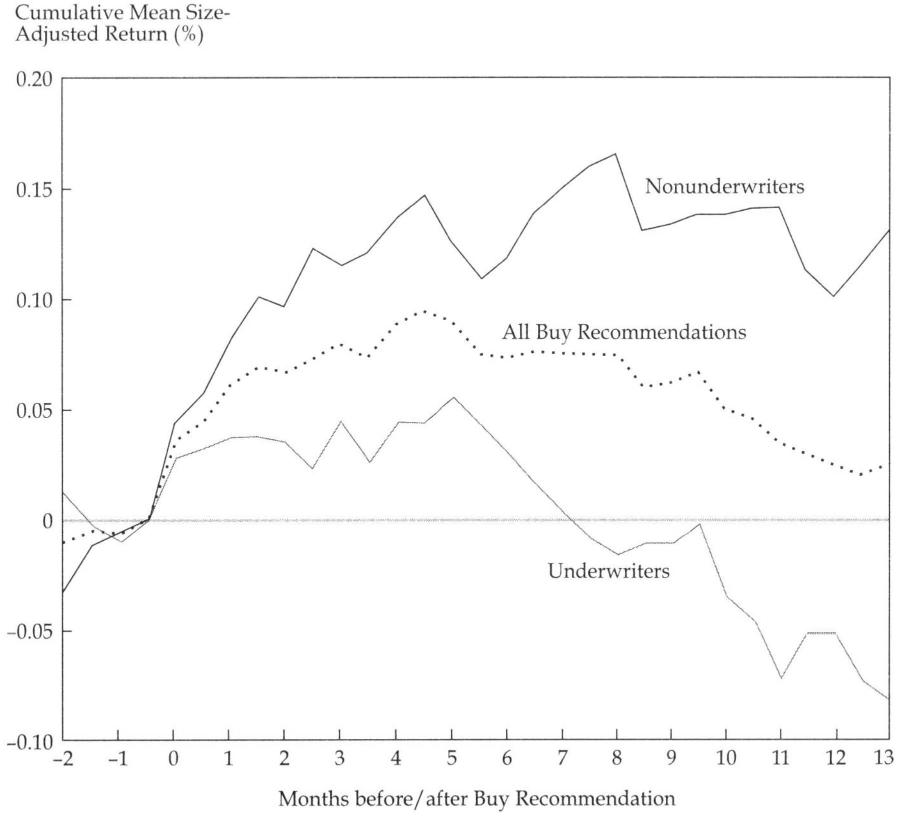

Source: Based on data from Michaely and Womack (1999).

value—about 12–15 percent risk-adjusted excess return over the next year. On the other hand, the recommendations by the underwriter analysts had positive risk-adjusted excess returns for the first four or five months but became negative after the seventh month. In fact, these underwriter recommendations have been known as "booster shots" in the financial press.

Our results also suggest that underwriters recommend stocks that have been underperforming. That is, many underwriter recommendations tended to occur after the IPO stock had been doing poorly for three or four weeks immediately prior to the recommendation, which suggests that underwriters were trying to bolster the stock's price when it was faltering. A similar pattern did not exist for the nonunderwriters, who were more likely to recommend stocks with strong momentum in the month before the recommendation.

Figure 4 reinforces the findings of Michaely and Womack on IPOs by showing the cumulative buy-and-hold returns over a 30-month horizon following the IPO date. Companies with recommendations made only by nonunderwriters had the best performance over the entire period. Thus, such recommendations were a valuable signal. This signal was especially strong for small companies that had few other sources of information. Figure 4 also shows that the next best category was companies recommended by both nonunderwriter and underwriter analysts. Companies with recommendations *only* from their underwriters (and no corroborating outside sources) had the worst cumulative performance. Our interpretation is that a recommendation of an analyst affiliated with the underwriter reflects a serious potential conflict of interest.

Is Underwriter Bias Intentional? A final issue is to determine whether this underwriter bias documented in Michaely and Womack is intentional or not. In the same study, because analysts face a conflict between truth telling and rent seeking, we conducted a survey of investment managers (who buy underwritings) and corporate finance executives of underwriters (who sell underwritings). One hundred percent of the investment managers who were surveyed indicated that they believed underwriter bias

Figure 4. Relative Performance of IPOs Recommended by Nonunderwriter and Underwriter Analysts, 1990–91

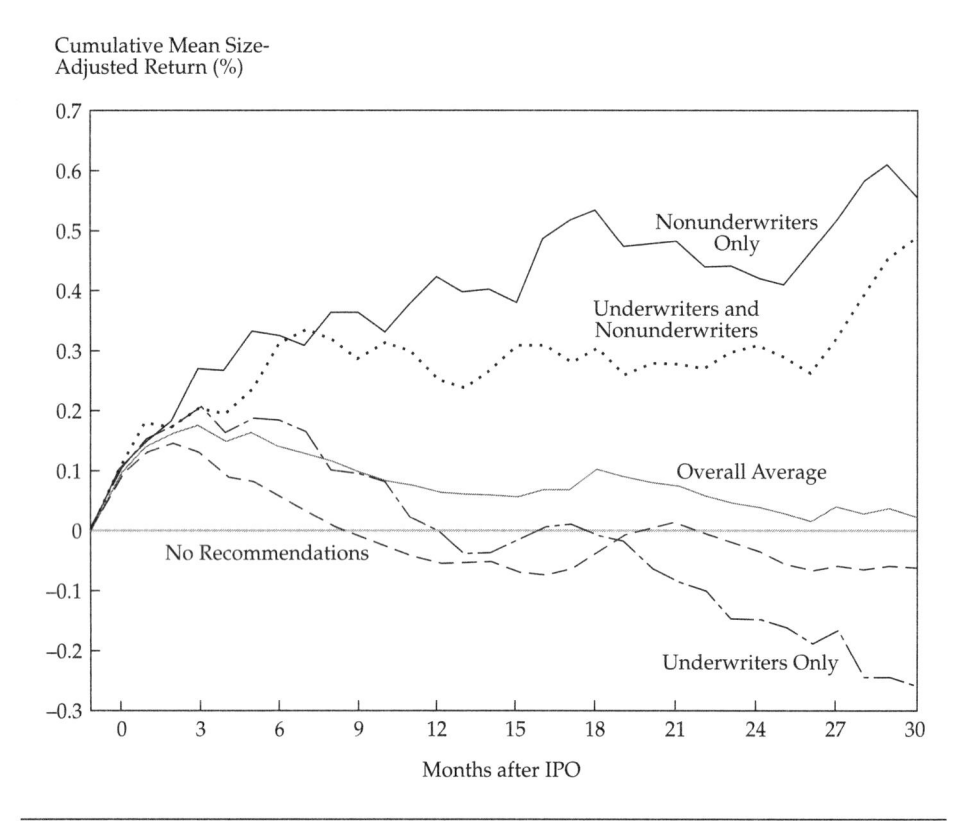

Note: Cumulative return begins at the IPO price.
Source: Based on data from Michaely and Womack (1999).

was intentional and reflected underwriters' self-interest. Even more damning, however, was the fact that more than half of the corporate finance executives at underwriting firms admitted that their analysts were not completely objective and that they were "cheating" a bit in terms of the value of their advice.

Despite the results of the survey, we find that many if not most analysts we survey truly believe that they are giving good advice. If so, why does the bias occur? A potential answer is a behavioral concept outlined by Kahneman and Lovallo (1993) that involves the framing of decisions like recommendations. They label the distinction the "inside view" versus the "outside view." The inside view is analogous to parents talking about their own children. Parents might never believe or even say that their kids are below average. Their children's teachers, however, might offer the "outside view" of someone who simply knows the hard, cold statistical facts of the issue.

Analysts appear to act very much like parents who "focus on the case at hand" (their children), whereas unaffiliated analysts are much more likely to "ignore the details of the case at hand" and focus "on the statistics of a class of cases chosen to be similar in relevant respects to the present one" (p. 25).

A Final Puzzle

This discussion has shown some evidence that the information provided by analysts adds value to the investment process, but the historical data suggest that a disconnect exists between potentially valuable information and the reportedly mediocre performance of active managers. Apparently, investors could use the information better and more wisely than they currently do. For example, in many firms, several weeks often pass between the time buy-side analysts learn of a new buy recommendation and the time they write an "action" report. The available evidence on analyst information suggests that, on average, the value of analyst information is short-lived. This finding is especially true for positive news. Thus, the delay in the investing process could be creating a barrier between potentially valuable information and performance.

Another piece of the puzzle shows that investors appear, initially, to discount or ignore negative information. This behavior may be because the new information is at odds with the presumably positive view that investors already hold (which is inherent in them as owners of the stock). They appear to be slow to adjust their valuations to negative information offered by the analysts. Interestingly, even ironically, this negative information is the most valuable information sell-side analysts offer because (when and if they give it) it is least likely to suffer from a conflict-of-interest bias.

Conclusion

Because analysts are human, they have human foibles and they are better at some tasks than others. Investors need to consider why analysts make certain errors. In order to make the best use of the information provided by analysts, investors should learn how to process the information and to sort out what is valuable and what is not.

Finally, several simple heuristics are appropriate for dealing with analyst information. When hearing a new recommendation, investors should ask four questions. First, is the pronouncement positive or negative? Negative information is more likely to be credible and valuable. Second, is the analyst's company the investment banker? Affiliated analysts appear to be poor forecasters of relative future results. Third, what aspect of this recommendation differs from the consensus view? Reiterating news and opinions already reflected in the market is likely of little value. Fourth, is the recommendation a "news" or an "undervaluation" story? Valuation-based recommendations usually have less impact and predictive ability than recommendations predicting future changes in the business.

Question and Answer Session

Kent L. Womack

Question: How do stocks that analysts recommend perform over the long term?

Womack: Over the long term, no evidence exists of abnormal performance for sell recommendations beyond the effect I showed in the first six months or so. For buy recommendations, the effect is even shorter, only one or two months. One must appreciate, however, that the statistical power to detect longer-term good performance is weak. We cannot rule out that the information may be valuable beyond the limited time frames I mentioned, but I know of no *statistical* evidence that it is.

Question: Do you know of any studies of the value of the recommendations of influential analysts, such as members of the *Institutional Investor* All-America Research Team, versus the average analyst? Are the All-America analysts better; do they have a bigger effect?

Womack: Stickel (1992) looked at this particular issue in the early 1990s and concluded that All-America analysts' forecasts of EPS are more accurate more often than those of other analysts. Furthermore, although his examination of stock returns immediately after large upward forecasts led him to conclude that All-America analysts affect prices more than other analysts do, he found almost no difference in returns after large downward revisions. Overall, his results suggest a positive relation between reputation and performance. It would be interesting to review similar data about their recommendations.

Question: Are the new buy recommendations based mostly on valuation, whereas the new sell recommendations are based mostly on new information?

Womack: In a broad sense, my preliminary pilot study found that 40 percent of the new buy recommendations have a valuation characteristic as the main issue and about another 40 percent involve breaking news or anticipated forthcoming events. For the remaining 20 percent, a financial change, such as restructuring, or other issues are the focus.

Question: Does any difference exist for regional versus national companies in terms of recommendations?

Womack: The size of the company results in a dramatic difference in how the market responds to a new piece of information. A recent working paper compared the national brokerage firms with regional firms. The regional firms are much more likely to analyze smaller stocks. Smaller stocks also respond more vigorously to these recommendations than do the large-cap stocks that national firms might recommend. So, a size bias exists that is hard to eliminate.

Question: Does the jargon of ratings, such as a buy versus a strong buy, make a difference in recommendations?

Womack: Not to my knowledge. No distinguishing characteristic seems to make much of a difference among the various nomenclatures given to buy ratings. A substantial difference exists between the "accumulate" or "attractive" (above average) rating and the buy rating in terms of the immediate impact and the one- or two-month drift. Buy ratings have much more clout.

Investor Overreaction and Contrarian Strategies

David N. Dreman
Chair and Chief Investment Officer
Dreman Value Management, L.L.C.

> Contrarian strategies provide investors with an opportunity to profit from different forms of investor overreaction in securities markets—"best" versus "worst" stocks, winners versus losers, initial public offerings, or seasoned equity offerings. The key to profiting from these strategies is to understand why the overreaction occurred and to avoid making cognitive and other psychological errors that have deceived other investors and prompted them to participate in the latest market bubble or mania.

Financial history is replete with examples of how seemingly rational people abandoned their senses and allowed market fundamentals to lead them to overreact or underreact to specific events or circumstances in financial markets. If investors can understand what leads to overreaction and underreaction and accurately predict when these phenomena occur, then they can develop strategies to profit from such market conditions. To do so, investors need to understand what types of cognitive and other psychological errors can lead them into the garden of tulipmania.

This presentation focuses on the significant body of research on the different types of investor over- and underreaction. The key questions are whether overreaction really occurs and, if so, when and why it takes place. The final section addresses manifestations of overreaction in terms of bubbles and panics in today's markets.

Investor Overreaction

Investor overreaction refers to the systematic over- or underpricing of stocks when measured, for example, by price-to-earnings ratio (P/E), price-to-book value (P/B), price to cash flow (P/CF), or dividend yield (P/D). A well-known type of approach that tries to take advantage of investor overreaction is a contrarian strategy. The idea underlying this strategy is that out-of-favor stocks significantly outperform the market.

The literature on contrarian strategies goes back to the 1960s. For example, Nicholson (1960, 1968), McWilliams (1966), and Miller and Widmann (1966) published research about the superior returns of low-P/E stocks. Research on contrarian strategies waned during the early 1970s when the theory of efficient markets was developing. The 1980s saw a revival of interest about investor overreaction, and interest has increased in the 1990s.

Several theories focus on investor overreaction. For example, Basu (1977, 1978, 1983) investigated the "price ratio hypothesis," in which the market underprices low-P/E stocks relative to their fundamental value. He suggested that investors tend to overreact to the mediocre prospects of low-P/E stocks by setting their prices too low, but investors overreact to high-P/E stocks' superior visibility by driving their prices too high.

Dreman (1977, 1979, 1982, 1998) extended the theory to other types of investments. The general thesis is that investors react to events in a predictable fashion. That is, investors consistently overvalue the prospects of the "best" (favored) investments and undervalue those of the "worst" (out-of-favor) investments. They extrapolate positive or negative outlooks well into the future, pushing prices of favored investments to excessive premiums and out-of-favor investments to discounts. After the mispricing, the worst investments outperform the market and the best investments lag the market as the prices of both revert to a more average valuation. Somewhere along the way, an event trigger, such as an earnings surprise, changes investors' perceptions, and mean reversion of stock prices occurs. This perceptual change causes the best stocks to underperform the market and worst stocks to outperform.

Fama and French's landmark 1992 study was a major about-face for the efficient market school. Whereas previous researchers concluded that contrarian strategies did not work or worked only because of higher risk, Fama and French found that low-P/B and low-P/E stocks beat the market. They also found that beta, a traditional measure of risk, was not correlated with return. That is, higher-beta portfolios did not give higher returns; lower-beta portfolios did not give lower returns.

Lakonishok, Shleifer, and Vishny (1994) examined several contrarian strategies and found that risk did not explain returns. They noted that stocks with low P/B and low price-to-sales (P/S) values did significantly better than those that had a high P/B and high P/S.

Dreman and Berry (1995b) found that positive earnings surprises sent prices of out-of-favor (low-P/E) stocks sharply higher and negative surprises sent prices of favored (high-P/E) stocks sharply lower. The authors referred to such surprises as event triggers, noting that they cause changes in investors' perceptions. Further, reinforcing events—positive surprises on favored stocks and negative surprises on out-of-favor stocks—caused little or no change in investor perception and had a minimal effect on stock price. The net result was above-market performance for the worst stocks and below-market performance for the best stocks—a result consistent with mispricing prior to earnings surprises. They also found that low-P/E and high-P/E stocks each experienced the same frequency and size of surprises, further supporting the hypothesis that investor perceptions lie at the root of the asymmetrical response to surprise. In addition, the above-market returns for low-P/E stocks continued for five years or more.

An important issue is how contrarian strategies work over time. Dreman (1998) measured average annual returns for low-P/E, low-P/B, low-P/CF, and low-P/D stocks over the 1970–98 period, as shown in **Figure 1**. The market had a 15.1 percent compound return, and all four groups outperformed the market as follows: low P/E, 18.5 percent; low P/B, 18.2 percent; low P/CF, 17.5 percent; low P/D, 16.3 percent. The behavioral question is not whether these strategies worked, as they obviously did, but why they worked.

Types of Overreaction. Although the basic principle of overreaction is widely familiar to investors, the phenomenon can have different manifestations:

■ *Winners and losers*. One type of overreaction involves winners and losers. De Bondt and Thaler (1985, p. 795) hypothesized that "if stock prices systematically overshoot, then their reversal should be predictable from past return data alone." They found that extreme "losers" (stocks with the lowest returns) beat the market in the next period and extreme winners lagged the market. De Bondt and Thaler were not interested in simple overreactions in analysts' forecasts or temporary or minor overreactions in a quarter or a six-month period. Instead, they were looking for overreactions that hold up for long periods. Theoretically, investors can systematically use such overreactions to enhance portfolio returns.

■ *Junk bonds*. Hickman (1958) and Atkinson (1967) examined another type of overreaction. They found that junk bonds, despite their higher default risk, systematically outperformed investment-grade bonds. The findings of these two studies suggest that investors tend to pay too little for a diversified portfolio of junk bonds relative to quality bonds.

■ *Stocks with earnings deficits*. Research conducted by Marine Midland Bank (1968) found that stocks with earnings deficits in one year tended to outperform the market. This finding is not well documented, however, and the age of the study raises the question of whether the same pattern would hold today.

■ *Initial public offerings*. Ritter (1991) and Loughran and Ritter (1995) studied 5,000 initial public offerings between 1970 and 1990. Although IPO prices increased significantly on the first day of trading, compounded average returns for the subsequent five-year holding periods were 15.7 percent for the IPO stocks versus 66.5 percent for the market. The median IPO return, however, was –39.0 percent. Thus, IPOs significantly underperformed the market in the long term.

■ *Seasoned equity offerings*. Loughran and Ritter (1995, 1997) also investigated seasoned equity offerings. They found that companies making seasoned equity offerings significantly underperformed the market. Companies most often made secondary offerings after a period of exceptional operating performance, but their profitability declined significantly thereafter. They noted that the market's expectations for companies using secondary offerings were too high. This effect was observed for companies of all sizes but was especially strong for small companies.

■ *Bubbles and crashes in the laboratory*. Smith (1992) and his colleagues at the University of Arizona conducted some interesting work in experimental economics. They set up a situation in which stocks paid a set average dividend and trading took place over a set number of time periods. A group of investors was allowed to buy or sell stock, knowing that they would get a well-defined average dividend during 15 trading periods. Using these experimental securities markets, Smith documented enormous price bubbles and crashes. Translating the results to the DJIA would result in 50–75 percent swings in the index. Porter and Smith (1994), Smith, Suchanek, and Williams (1988), and Caginalp, Porter, and Smith (forthcoming 1999) conducted similar studies that reinforced Smith's initial findings.

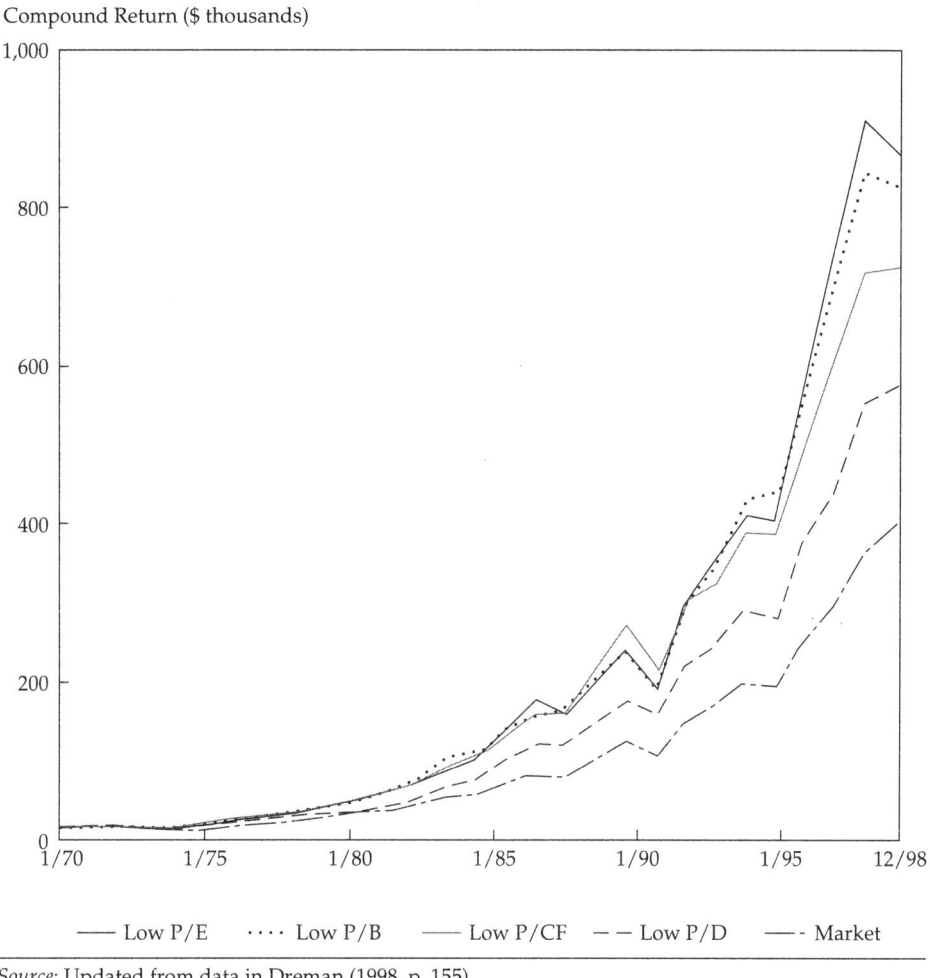

Figure 1. Compound Returns for Contrarian Strategies, 1970–98

Source: Updated from data in Dreman (1998, p. 155).
Note: Based on initial investment of $10 thousand in 1970 with annual rebalancing.

Controversy. Investor overreaction has generated much controversy because the efficient market hypothesis rules out overreaction. According to EMH, rational investors should step in to price stocks correctly. The subject of overreaction, particularly in the original contrarian strategies, troubled EMH advocates because if investors could get systematically higher returns by using a contrarian strategy, then markets were inefficient.

Some researchers, such as Ball (1978) and Fama and French (1995, 1996), have contended that any overreaction or any extra return for contrarian strategies has to result from higher risk assumed with those strategies. Evidence of this higher risk, however, has not been found.

Other researchers, such as Banz and Breen (1986), argued that the results associated with contrarian stocks are caused by data biases or faulty methodology. Many studies—including Fama and French (1992), Lakonishok, Shleifer, and Vishny, and Dreman and Berry (1995b)—addressed these concerns.

Some scholars, such as Reinganum (1981), argued that the low-P/E phenomenon was a small-capitalization phenomenon and that without small caps, no excess return would exist. Basu (1983), Fama and French (1992), Dreman (1990, 1998), and others refuted this argument.

Although research has not supported most of the criticisms associated with risk adjustment, a problem still exists with overreaction. The problem is that researchers have never directly measured overreaction. Researchers have measured only the superior or inferior returns of best and worst stocks, bonds, and other investments. Although research shows that contrarian strategies may result in superior returns, those returns could result from factors other than overreaction. For example, if the fundamentals of the best stocks deteriorate substantially and those of the worst stocks improve, no overreaction exists and the market is acting rationally. Markets would act as they should under EMH assumptions. That is, investors should pay less for favored stocks to adjust for the poorer fundamentals; they should pay more for out-of-favor stocks to adjust for the improved fundamentals. No definitive proof demonstrates that overreaction is a psychological, not a rational, phenomenon. To make such a finding would require linking changes in fundamentals to the superior returns of value stocks.

Investor Underreaction

Many event studies find underreaction to events (also called "drift") instead of overreaction. For example, Bernard and Thomas (1989, 1990) and Abarbanell and Bernard (1992) define underreaction as the phenomenon in which analysts do not correctly adjust their earnings estimates immediately. These researchers find autocorrelation between earnings surprises—that is, a positive surprise in one quarter increases the probability of another positive surprise in the next three quarters. They also report similar results for negative surprises. Their conclusion is that analysts do not make sufficient revisions after an earnings surprise. In other words, analysts underreact to new information.

Michaely, Thaler, and Womack (1995) show that prices following dividend cuts and initiations do not adjust rapidly but could take two years or more to adjust. If companies raise their dividends, their stock prices go up for the following two years; if companies cut dividends, their stock prices go down for two years or more. The market, therefore, appears slow to adjust to information, which indicates underreaction. Ikenberry, Rankine, and Stice (1996) also found that above-market returns continue for as long as three years after stock splits.

When Overreaction Occurs

If overreaction occurs, when does it occur? Some studies do not clearly indicate whether the past event or the response to the event is the overreaction. This lack of specificity has caused some confusion in the literature.

Dreman and Lufkin (forthcoming 1999) investigated this question. The goal of this study was to show whether the basis of overreaction was the changing fundamentals of best and worst stocks or psychological factors. Both financial academics and practitioners generally agree that a company's underlying fundamentals, particularly earnings growth, determine price movements over time. Specifically, we investigated five important fundamentals: earnings growth, cash flow growth, sales growth, return on equity, and profit margin. The study compared returns of best and worst stocks with the movements of their underlying fundamentals to determine the cause of the above- or below-market returns.

To determine whether an overreaction occurred, the study looked at the relationship between annual market-adjusted returns five years before and five years after portfolio formation ($t = 0$) and the fundamentals in the same periods. Fundamentals were actually measured for 10 years prior to portfolio formation. Using the Compustat 1500 (the 1,500 largest companies in the Compustat database in terms of market value of equity at the beginning of each calendar year), the authors examined the pattern for stock returns and for each fundamental during the five-year periods starting in 1973 through the five years beginning in 1994.

The market-adjusted returns of high-P/B (favored) and low-P/B (out-of-favor) stocks are virtually mirror images of each other, as **Figure 2** shows. (The line labeled zero represents the market. Because the average market return over the 1973–98 period was about 17 percent, the zero line actually represents about 17 percent.) High-P/B stocks had above-market returns during the period before portfolio formation but below-market returns for the subsequent period. In fact, their annual market-adjusted returns rose from 12 percent to about 20 percent in the year before portfolios are formed and then fell sharply to –2 or –3 percent after portfolio formation—a 23 percent change in returns in only one year.

Low-P/B stocks had an opposite pattern of returns compared with the high-P/B stocks. Out-of-favor stocks had below-market returns before portfo-

Figure 2. Market-Adjusted Performance of High- and Low-P/B Stocks, 1973–98

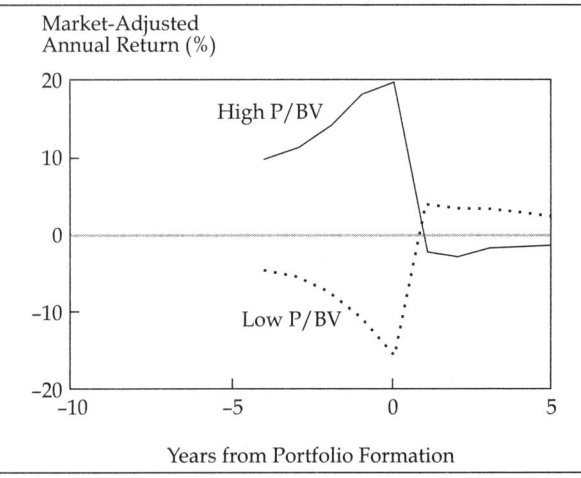

Source: Based on data from Dreman and Lufkin (forthcoming 1999).

lio formation but above-market returns afterward. Their average market-adjusted returns fell from about –5 percent to –15 percent during the period before portfolio formation and then rose sharply to about 3 or 4 percent above market after portfolio formation.

The relationship between the market-adjusted returns for the high-P/B and low-P/B stocks and each of the five fundamentals, as shown in **Figure 3**, provides several interesting observations:

- The value of each fundamental (cash flow growth, sales growth, earnings growth, return on equity, and profit margin) was higher for the high-P/B stocks than for the market throughout the 1973–98 period. For instance, cash flow growth of the highest-P/B stocks increases steadily from 18 percent in the 10th year before portfolio formation to 23 percent in the final year before portfolio formation, well above the market's cash flow

Figure 3. Fundamentals for High- and Low-P/B Stocks, 1973–98

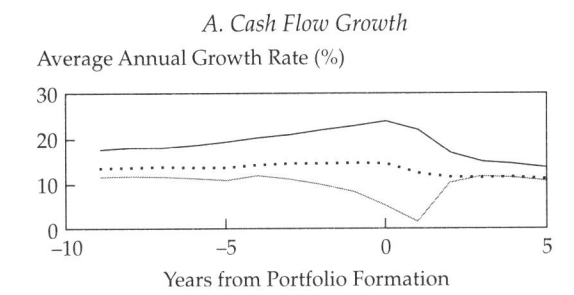

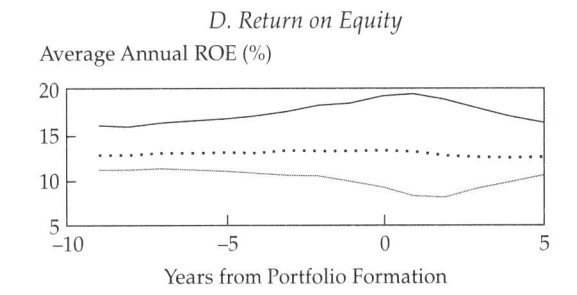

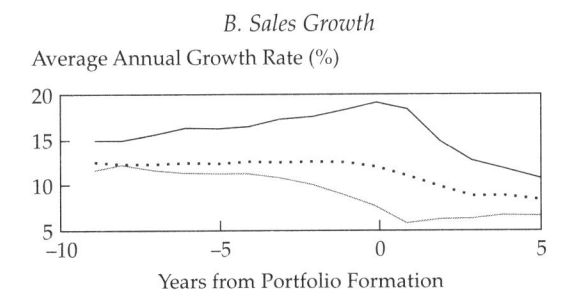

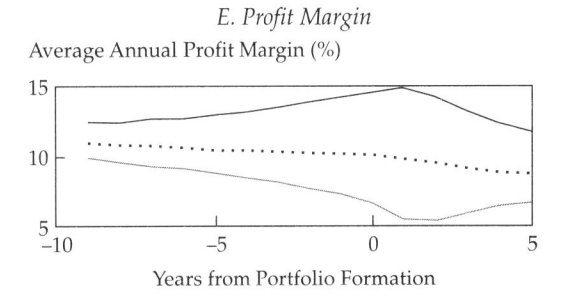

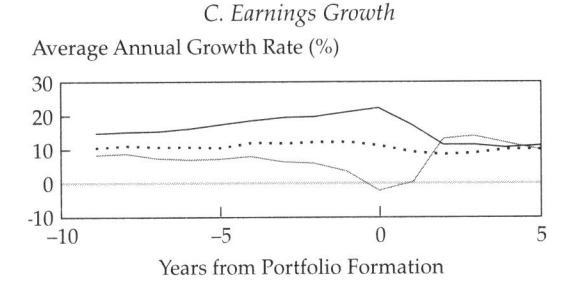

A. Cash Flow Growth

B. Sales Growth

C. Earnings Growth

D. Return on Equity

E. Profit Margin

—— High P/BV ···· Market —— Low P/BV

Source: Based on data from Dreman and Lufkin (forthcoming 1999).

growth of about 12 percent. Although cash flow growth of favored stocks slows some after portfolio formation, it is always above that of the market and the low-P/B group.

- The value of three fundamentals (growth in sales, return on equity, and profit margin) was lower for the low-P/B stocks than for the market throughout the 1973–98 period. Cash flow growth and earnings growth were also lower than the market before portfolios were formed and near or below market afterwards. Sales growth of the lowest-P/B stocks, for example, starts out about even with the market (about 12 percent a year), then drops almost 50 percent until the first year after portfolios are formed and remains well below both the market and the high-P/B group for the next four years.

- There is no reversal in fundamentals to match the reversals in returns. Before portfolio formation, investors could see that the high-P/B stocks had superior fundamentals to the market as much as 10 years in the past. But going forward, high-P/B stocks continued to have the best fundamentals even as their returns took a precipitous dive. For example, in the first year after portfolio formation, cash flow of the high-P/B group still grows rapidly, nudging down slightly to 22 percent annually from 23 percent in the prior year. Nevertheless, the cash flow growth of the best stocks is double that of the market and about 20 times that of the out-of-favor issues. At the same time, the returns of the best stocks plummet 23 percent in the first year following portfolio formation and continue to underperform the market for the next four years. Fundamentals, then, clearly do not support the dramatic turnaround in the returns of high-P/B stocks.

- Low-P/B stocks again show a mirror image. For example, after declining steadily for a number of years, cash flow growth for the low-P/B group drops even more sharply, from 5 percent to 1 percent, in the same year that returns for these stocks soar from 15 percent below market to 4 percent above market. The acceleration of deteriorating fundamentals clearly cannot be the cause of an abrupt 19 percent increase in the returns of low-P/B stocks. And as low-P/B stocks continue to outperform both the market and the high-P/B group for the next four years, their cash flow growth, although improving moderately in Years 2–5, never exceeds that of the market and never catches up with that of the most favored stocks.

- These results are typical of those found for other measures in the study: low and high P/E, P/CF (not shown here), and P/B stocks have huge swings in returns with little or no change in fundamentals to back them up.

Overall, Figures 2 and 3 show nearly identical results. Favored stocks substantially underperformed out-of-favor stocks during the five-year period after portfolio formation. During the same period, favored stocks experienced little or no decrease in fundamentals—and in some cases even an increase—and had much lower market-adjusted returns. Conversely, out-of-favor stocks experienced almost no increase in fundamentals—and in some cases even a continued decrease—coupled with much higher market-adjusted returns. In the absence of any consistent link between fundamentals and returns, the cause of the major price reversals must be psychological—or more specifically, investor overreaction.

Reconciling Overreaction with Underreaction

Overreaction and underreaction are part of the same process, with overreaction occurring before portfolio formation and underreaction occurring afterward. We at Dreman Value Management view overreaction as the overpricing of favored stocks and underpricing of out-of-favor issues, which takes place at and before portfolio formation.

Underreaction can be seen in the slow correction process documented above for the Year 1 to Year 5 period. Stock prices, like analysts' forecasts, do not adjust fully or quickly to new information. In our view, this slow correction process is the normal consequence of the overreaction that has taken place in the prior period. Investors first overreact by steeply overpricing favored stocks and as sharply underpricing out-of-favor stocks. They then underreact by failing to correct the prior mispricing quickly.

Perceptions of stocks change—but not instantaneously, as efficient market theory hypothesizes. Rather, the process is a slow one. The belief in the inevitable 20 percent plus growth of an Avon Products or a Polaroid Corporation in the early 1970s or in the 50 percent plus earnings growth of a Dell Computer Corporation or many of the Internet stocks in the late 1990s does not change overnight. The transition in thinking often takes years to be completed, which causes the five years of overblown returns for favored stocks in the $t = -5$ to $t = 0$ period and the equally long period of underperformance thereafter.

Table 1 shows cumulative market-adjusted returns before and after portfolio formation ($t = 0$) for stocks in the low and high P/E, P/CF, and P/B quintile groupings. Portfolios with low P/E, P/CF, and P/B have negative market-adjusted returns

Table 1. Compound Market-Adjusted Return before and after Portfolio Formation, 1973–98

Indicator	−4	−3	−2	−1	0	+1	+2	+3	+4	+5
Low P/B	−4.9%	−12.7%	−24.5%	−45.5%	−79.4%	3.5%	8.3%	14.9%	23.3%	33.3
High P/B	9.5	25.8	54.2	104.9	187.1	−2.6	−7.4	−11.8	−17.5	−26.5
Low P/CF	−3.8	−8.8	−14.8	−24.4	−54.1	2.6	5.4	9.6	15.8	22.3
High P/CF	8.2	19.1	35.5	65.1	128.1	−3.4	−9.8	−16.5	−23.0	−30.1
Low P/E	−4.1	−6.1	−4.8	−2.9	−20.5	4.0	8.6	14.9	23.7	33.5
High P/E	4.5	8.4	14.8	25.1	58.7	−3.5	−9.4	−16.0	−23.3	−30.9

Note: One-year returns, so for example, −4 represents the return data for the year starting five years before portfolio formation.

before portfolio formation but positive market-adjusted returns after portfolio formation. Portfolios with high P/E, P/CF, and P/B have the opposite pattern of market-adjusted returns. Table 1 suggests that overreaction and underreaction are part of the ebb and flow of market returns as well as a catalyst for bubbles and panics.

Bubbles and Panics

If the overreaction and underreaction phenomena discussed so far represent the neurotic side of the market, then bubbles and panics are the psychotic side. Bubbles are unjustifiable, sharp upward deviations from fundamental values. Panics are just the opposite—unjustifiable, sharp downward deviations from fundamentals. Ominously, certain areas of the market in 1999, at least from a value manager's point of view, may be in the midst of a major bubble.

Recent Bubbles. In bubbles, many different rationalizations exist for the high prices. In 1999, some of these rationalizations include "this market is unique," "no period has ever seen the technology advancements of this time," "this is a new era," and "there is a shortage of stocks" (i.e., the market is "liquidity driven"). Investors are told that a nearly unlimited amount of money is pouring into IRAs and that 7.5 million day traders "must keep stocks moving higher." Another popular view is that existing valuation methods are inappropriate for valuing some types of issues, such as Internet stocks.

Such rationalizations are not new. Almost identical reasoning was at work in previous bubbles: the great stock market crash of 1929, the technology bubbles of the 1960s, and the IPO bubbles of the late 1970s and early 1980s. Recent bubbles include those in Asia, Russia, Latin America, IPOs, and possibly the Internet. In fact, more bubbles have occurred in the post–World War II period than in any other period of financial history.

What is interesting about the recent bubbles is that they involve large flows of foreign capital. When the Russian market went up 100 percent several years ago, U.S. investors, and possibly some from Europe and Asia, did about 90 percent of the trading. The same phenomenon is true for the Asian bubble and, to some extent, the Latin American bubble.

A popular question is whether a bubble exists for Internet stocks. **Table 2** shows recent prices for some of the favorite Internet stocks as well as the values derived for those stocks using earnings discount models. The models assumed that earnings would grow at 50 percent for the first three years, 25 percent for the next five years, 20 percent for the next six years, 15 percent for another five years, and 7.5 percent (the historical rate of the S&P 500 Index since 1980) thereafter. If met, these growth rates will be the fastest in U.S. history for any industry. Two discount rates were applied. The 15 percent rate includes 5.9 percent on long government bonds plus a 9.1 percent risk premium; the 20 percent rate includes a 14.1 percent risk premium.

For example, in July 1999, eBay stock sold for $150 per share and had a P/E of 1,663. Based on the 15 percent and 20 percent discount factors, eBay's estimated value is $12 or $5, respectively. The stock appears highly overpriced. In general, the current prices of Internet stocks appear very high using the earnings discount model.

Causes of Bubbles and Panics. Over the past several decades, psychologists and other social scientists have produced a wealth of research that can help us understand how and why bubbles and panics take place. Three important explanations of these phenomena derive from cognitive psychology, group dynamics, and contagion theory.

■ *Cognitive psychology.* One approach for explaining bubbles and panics is cognitive psychology. This area of research focuses on heuristic biases. Heuristics are mental rules of thumb that help people function despite being bombarded by billions of in-

Table 2. Valuation of Internet Stocks, July 1, 1999

Company	Recent Price	P/E	Present Value of Discounted Future Earnings[a] 15 Percent	20 Percent
Realnetworks	$ 78	1,947	$ 5	$ 2
eBay	150	1,663	12	5
Broadcast.com	136	971[b]	14	6
Yahoo!	177	933	26	11
Mindspring	46	360[b]	17	8
Quest Communications	33	303[c]	13	5
Ameritrade	104	258[c]	55	24
At Home	55	250	23	9
E*TRADE Securities	40	248[c]	16	7
America Online	112	179	85	37

[a]Discount rates are calculated as follows: 15 percent rate includes 5.9 percent on long government bonds plus a 9.1 percent risk premium; 20 percent rate includes a 14.1 percent risk premium.
[b]Based on 1999 estimate (negative trailing earnings).
[c]Based on 2000 estimate (negative trailing earnings and 1999 estimate).

puts. Someone driving down a road faces many thousands of distractions but can remain focused on the road and get to the destination. In this case, the heuristics used by the driver work very well. In financial markets, however, heuristic biases can lead investors astray. Cognitive psychologists have found that people are poor statistical processors when they use heuristics. Three major categories of heuristic biases or mental shortcuts with significance for behavioral finance are availability, representativeness, and anchoring. All three result in major decision-making errors.

Tversky and Kahneman (1974, p. 11) defined availability as a mental rule of thumb by which people "assess the probabilities of an event by the ease with which instances or occurrences can be brought to mind." For example, during the 1990 Persian Gulf crisis, markets dropped sharply and investors feared an oil embargo. This fear resulted from events in the Middle East reminding investors of the oil embargoes in 1973 and 1980. Although 1990 differed from previous periods with oil embargoes because the world was awash in oil, the heuristic made investors fear an oil shortage: Oil and airline stock prices fell by as much as one third. Another example of the availability heuristic is the stock market crash of 1987, which immediately brought the idea of depression to the minds of investors. Although the United States has experienced many crashes and made quick recoveries, an association existed between crash and depression because of the 1929–32 experience. The availability bias makes this association an easy one, resulting in the heuristic error.

A subcategory of availability is recency and saliency. Investors tend to forget the past because of their attraction to the short term. The more recent and salient an event, the more likely that investors will exaggerate the long-term probabilities of the continuation of that event. For example, if investors buy Yahoo! stock and it goes up 20-fold, they tend to forget that this dramatic increase in price contradicts long-term valuation norms or that people have lost money on many similar exciting concepts in the past. Other examples include computer leasing companies in the 1967 market, Levitz Furniture in 1972, or personal computer companies in the 1980–82 period.

Another heuristic bias is representativeness. The law of small numbers, put forth by Tversky and Kahneman (1974), is a form of representativeness and states that, although large numbers are representative of something that will happen in a large statistical pool, small numbers may not provide a representative sample or may have major deviations from the sample. One example is a market timer. Statistically, most market timers do not do very well, but a market timer who makes a good call, such as Joseph Granville in the 1970s or Elaine Garzerelli in the 1987 stock market crash, is revered. Investors tend to remember the few good calls and forget about all the not-so-good advice.

Several other subcategories of representativeness exist. One example is the misperception of probabilities, which suggests that investors assign inappropriate probabilities to expected events. Another type of representativeness, the input/output fallacy, states that investors have an overenhancement of confidence based on the consistency of inputs. In other words, consistent inputs allow greater predictability than inconsistent ones. Tests have shown, for example, that people are far more confident that a student will regularly have a B average if he or she has two Bs rather than an A and a C, although the belief is not statistically valid (see Kahneman and Tversky 1973). Or if a company shows 20 percent earnings growth for five straight years, it will receive a much higher valuation than a similar company that grows with the same cumulative changes but has less consistent year-to-year results.

A third simplifying heuristic is known as anchoring. In a complex situation, such as the marketplace, investors choose some natural starting point, such as a stock's current price, as a first cut at its value and make adjustments from there. But the adjustments are typically insufficient. Thus, an investor in the spring of 1999 might have thought a price of $62 was too high for Ameritrade, a leading online broker, and that $50 was more appropriate. But Ameritrade was grossly overvalued at $50 and dropped to $17 later in the year.

- *Group dynamics.* The phenomenon of group dynamics often occurs in investment committees, when managers receive pressure to move with the flow because respected professionals are making popular investment decisions. If a manager does not invest in these stocks and their prices continue to rise while the manager's portfolio underperforms, he or she faces enormous pressure to change. Analysts face the same career pressures when they recommend unpopular stocks while other issues are rapidly rising.

- *Contagion theory.* Other research focusing on why bubbles get so far out of hand comes from the new field of contagion theory. In his recent book *Thought Contagion* (1996) and in follow-up work (forthcoming 1999), Aaron Lynch describes the causes of the current technology phenomenon.

Contagion theory likens the spread of a sweeping concept (or "meme") to an epidemic. The spread of contagion depends on the number of investors already infected and the ease of contacting other individuals who will become new hosts. The larger the number of hosts and the greater the ease of transmission of the idea to the unafflicted, the larger the mania can become. Specifically, Lynch describes three primary factors affecting the spread of memes: transmissivity (how easily ideas are transmitted to a new host or, in this case, a new investor), receptivity (how easily a new investor can become infected with these ideas), and longevity (how long a person remains a host after becoming infected).

For example, with millions of people trading technology stocks and IPOs, constant coverage by the TV market channels, the press, and other media, and dozens of Internet and other stock chat rooms and billboards, the transmission rate is startlingly high. Add to this the profits many are currently making, despite many experts saying that Internet stocks were overpriced several years ago. Given the circumstances, it is easy to see just how powerful the forces are that pull additional investors into the mania.

Longevity explains how an investor can stay infected for a long time as well as infecting new hosts who pass it on until it can assume mania proportions. These factors encourage the host to continue holding or investing in Internet stocks and to talk to other people about them. The bubble thus has the possibility of being fueled for many months or even years.

Conclusion

Extensive research on overreaction and underreaction provides investors with the following important conclusions to keep in mind to either take advantage of underreaction or avoid overreacting in equities markets.

- Favored stocks significantly outperformed the market while out-of-favor stocks sharply underperformed in the five years before portfolio formation.
- Above-market returns for out-of-favor stocks and below-market returns for favored stocks begin after portfolio formation and continue long into the future.
- Over time, fundamentals are remarkably consistent: Favored stocks have superior fundamentals, and out-of-favor stocks have inferior fundamentals both before and after portfolio formation. Little or no change in fundamentals exists to support the dramatic changes in returns occurring in the first year after portfolio formation. In fact, the returns of out-of-favor stocks, for example, can change from underperforming the market by 15 percent in the year before portfolio formation to outperforming by 4 percent the following year, even as growth rates for those stocks continue to decline. Therefore, no fundamental superiority exists for worst stocks that justifies their superior performance after portfolio formation, nor is there any inferiority in the fundamentals of best stocks to justify their below-market performance.
- Underreaction, or event drift, occurs after portfolio formation and is part of the total overreaction process.

Statistics overwhelmingly bear out the fact that contrarian strategies and other overreaction strategies work because of the fact that investors move away from fundamentals. Still, investors have to avoid cognitive, contagion, and group psychological effects that may deceive them into totally abandoning market fundamentals and prompt them to participate in market bubbles and panics.

Practical Issues in Equity Analysis

Question and Answer Session

David N. Dreman

Question: Why have value stocks performed so badly during the past decade? Is the recent systematic underperformance, relative to other active managers, by active managers who use contrarian strategies a permanent change?

Dreman: Value strategies have recently performed worse than ever before, even worse than in the two-tier market of the early 1970s. In 1971 and 1972, value stocks underperformed growth stocks by 35 percent in two years. After the two-tier market, commencing in 1975, value outperformed growth for the next 10 years by more than 10 to 1, or 501 percent versus 43 percent. Although significant underperformance by value stocks does not happen often, maybe once or twice a generation, value investors have unfortunately experienced this phenomenon in recent years. Now is a difficult time to be a value manager, but the psychology of overreaction explains the striking dichotomy between growth and value performance in recent years—a dichotomy, I believe, that will reverse itself, perhaps sharply, in the next year or two.

The recent performance of value managers does not represent a fundamental change in valuation. Someone recently wrote a letter to *Forbes* saying that those who believe this change is not permanent are dinosaurs. Maybe today is different, but I have seen similar comments when researching other periods of major exuberance. People before the 1929 stock market crash thought that the market had entered a new era; today, people are talking of a new era again.

Question: What is your response to Kent Womack's[1] observation

[1] See Professor Womack's presentation in this proceedings.

that the market responds more favorably to the presumption that something new will happen than it does to lower valuation? Is that observation an example of overreaction, or does valuation even matter?

Dreman: Womack's figures show short-term performance relative to the longer-term performance discussed in this presentation. I define short term as a year or less. In Womack's presentation, the effects of the recommendations are largely gone after about six months. My research, as well as the research of others, suggests that some stocks outperform or underperform for as long as five years or more. Out-of-favor stocks outperformed favored stocks, on average, by about 5 or 6 percentage points a year. Valuations eventually rise, but they do not get there as quickly as investors want.

Question: Why is a person irrational to believe that all the new money going into the markets is driving up stock prices and will continue to do so?

Dreman: The question of liquidity is a fascinating one. In 1987, the popular view was that the market could not go down. In the summer of 1987, Salomon Brothers called a group of money managers together, and all of them thought that the market was liquidity driven and this fact could not change. The problem is that liquidity can change. For example, Dell might trade 125 million shares in a day, which it did recently, but that 125 million could go down to 10 million with a major change in investor expectations. The farther stocks stray from what most informed observers consider rational values, or values that have a basis in the fundamentals, the greater the danger of a major change.

Question: Do your studies show that contrarian investing is consistent for all sectors?

Dreman: Contrarian investing is consistent among sectors. Our research suggests that if an investor buys the lowest-multiple companies in an industry, the P/B or the P/E does not matter. These stocks outperform both their industry and the market by roughly 2 to 2.5 percentage points over time (Dreman and Lufkin 1997).

Question: What time frame do you recommend that a real contrarian investor use, and how can investors decide when to sell?

Dreman: We use a time frame of about two and a half to three years. If the stock does not at least match the market at that point, we sell it.

Question: Where do you see the greatest gaps in the behavioral finance literature?

Dreman: One gap involves group dynamics. For example, enormous pressure exists for analysts to recommend stocks in favored areas. If they do not, then they may face career problems. Another example of group dynamics is the two-tier market of the 1971–72 period, in which every major institution bought the so-called "Nifty Fifty" stocks. Institutions went on a buying spree to such a degree that the U.S. Senate Banking Committee held hearings on the matter. All of the major institutions told the committee that the Nifty Fifty were the only stocks to buy, just before they fell 90 percent in value. Other important areas that need more work include contagion theory and social psychology.

©2000, Association for Investment Management and Research

Global Equity Management and Valuation

M. Campbell Gunn
Managing Director and Chief Investment Officer
Meiji Dresdner Asset Management

> Global equity investors must decide whether to construct equity portfolios using macroeconomic analysis or global sector analysis. A macroeconomic approach can have major drawbacks, but to use sector analysis is to confront the potentially serious limitations of traditional valuation methods. Alternative methods, however, also have flaws, and the challenge for investors is to make the right trade-offs in developing an approach to suit their particular needs.

All global equity investors face the same important decision: Should global equity portfolios be constructed by looking at countries and determining country weightings through a process of macroeconomic analysis, or should they be constructed on a purely bottom-up basis with the emphasis, at least from a perspective of risk control, on global sectors? The way fund management firms answer this question determines not only how portfolios are constructed but also how the firms are organized.

In making cross-border comparisons of companies in the same sector, investors confront the shortcomings of traditional valuation measures and the problem created by differences in accounting standards. In response to this challenge, several competing valuation methods have emerged. Each of the new methods has devoted followers who maintain that their method is the "One True Way." Various brokerage houses have converted to one or more of these approaches. Not all fund managers are convinced by the new methods, and the majority prefer to use the traditional tools of the trade.

This presentation addresses both of these issues. The first section examines the countries-versus-sectors debate and concludes in favor of sectors. The second section reviews the problems with traditional valuation methods and evaluates the three main alternative approaches.

Global Equity Investing

In most global equity processes today, fund managers avoid making an explicit choice between country and sector allocations and use a mixture of both, although the tension between the top-down and the bottom-up approaches is not always creative.

Global Sectors versus Local Markets. Most fund management companies have grown, and are still structured, along geographical lines. Many are still dominated by local profit centers, rather than global and local product profit and loss statements. As the investment industry consolidates further, global versus local is the key issue for the emerging global asset management entities. In our own case, Meiji Dresdner Bank's global asset management business incorporates the formerly separate asset management entities of Thornton, Kleinwort Benson Investment Management, RCM, BIP Gestion, and Meisei Capital Management, as well as a number of German-based asset management businesses.

The traditional geographical structure tends to favor a global equity asset allocation process that is top-down in orientation. Top-down processes, being primarily concerned with macro factors, favor countries over sectors. This process can result in, say, the Tokyo office receiving an allocation of 12 percent of a model global portfolio even though the fund managers may not be able to find sufficiently attractive companies to fill the allocation.

Because the Tokyo fund managers are measured against their local benchmark, they proceed to over- or underallocate to sectors within it without reference to the quality of the businesses or sectors or to what European or U.S. equity fund managers are doing. If this process is then replicated in every overseas office, the result is a global portfolio with almost all of its global property exposure in one city in China, with both the best and the worst banks in the world and with an overweight position in global pharmaceuticals, which is the one sector every office wants to overweight.

In our own case, the imperative of integrating multiple offices and the bottom-up nature of the existing core global equity process forced us to move away from the geographic model. We now have a global equity team with members in every location who are separate and distinct from the local equity teams. They uplink ideas from local managers and download the resulting global model. By linking the regions through twice-daily conference calls, we have created a virtual global equity process that operates 24 hours a day.

Evaluating Risk. The realities of global investing favor portfolios with greater liquidity. About 2,000 companies worldwide have a market capitalization of more than US$2 billion, and most global investors select companies within this universe. In addition, the widespread adoption of global equity benchmarks, such as the MSCI World Index and the FT/S&P Actuaries World Index, have encouraged this concentration. As more money is managed with a global perspective, more capital is allocated to the leading global companies. As a result, there is a trend toward concentration on the largest, most liquid companies while smaller companies globally are underperforming.

A famous study by Roll (1992) found index volatility is a function of the industrial composition of the index. **Figure 1** shows that concentrated stock markets, such as South Africa and Hong Kong, have greater-than-average volatility. North American markets are at the opposite end of the spectrum. Japan's high volatility is attributed to the substantial cross-shareholdings among industry groups and the interconnectivity of the Japanese business model, which causes all Japanese companies to rise and fall together.

Roll also found that national index returns are composed of a weighted average of global sector index returns plus a country-specific disturbance factor. Global indexes of non-U.S. returns explain almost 40 percent of the volatility in a country's U.S.-dollar-denominated stock returns. Using a measure of the degree of global integration, Roll found that the most integrated global sectors were finance and consumer goods. Returns of non-U.S. finance and consumer goods companies were highly significant for each local market index. The least integrated sector was energy, which is a function of the different types of energy companies in each market—e.g., exploration versus downstream. European and Asian markets were found to be highly interrelated, whereas the United States was the least interrelated market globally.

Another way to look at Roll's findings is to consider the practical limitations of investing in only the top 2,000 global companies. For example, compare

Figure 1. Stock Index Volatility and Index Concentration

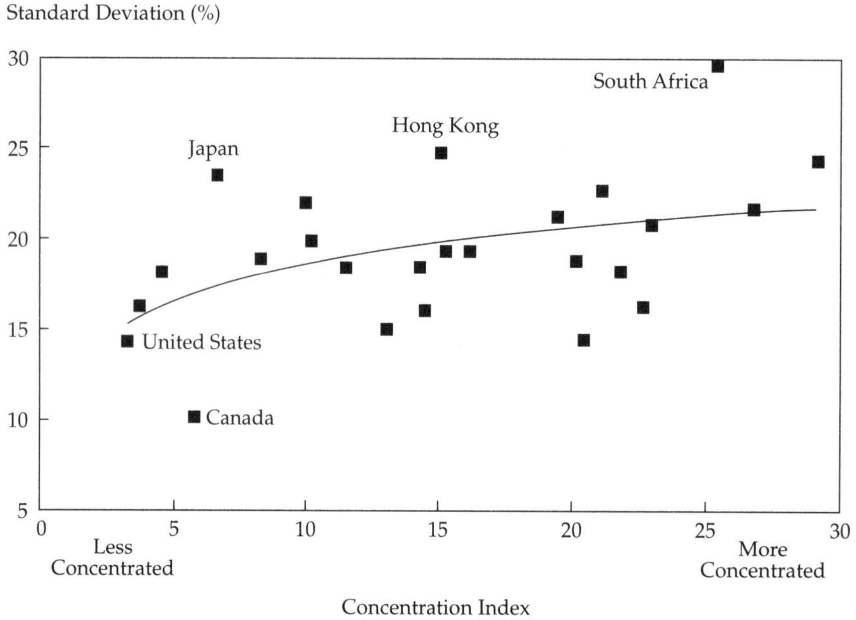

Source: Based on data from Roll (1992).

the cash flow internal rate of return (IRR) in excess of the local market discount rate with the premium that the market is prepared to pay above book value as a measure of value creation. The result is a snapshot of the investment opportunities available by country or sector, as shown in **Figure 2** for German and Japanese companies as of the beginning of 1999. The preferred quadrant is the bottom right, with a high positive IRR spread and moderate market-to-book value.

The median cash flow IRR spread in excess of the discount rate is –1.8 for the top Japanese companies and 1.0 for German companies, compared with the global median spread of 2.0. A diversified benchmark-oriented portfolio within either market would contain companies that were below the global mean, thus lowering the overall average for the global portfolio.

Although only 3 German and 13 Japanese companies occupy the bottom right quadrant, investing only in these companies would be unusual for a traditionally structured global equity portfolio. The local index tracking error would be substantial, and local managers' performance would most likely be measured against a local, rather than a global, benchmark.

From a sector perspective, the world looks very different and intra-sector and cross-sector comparisons are more meaningful. For example, compare the economics of the auto and technology industries. **Figure 3** shows that as of the beginning of 1999, Toyota Motor Corporation was a median performer within the auto sector but added no value; General Motors Corporation had a 10 percent positive spread but had the same relative value as Toyota. Microsoft Corporation's economics were clearly recognized by the market, but at this time, investing in Adobe Systems or Sun Microsystems looked more rewarding. The final step is to be able to compare the relative merits of General Motors and Adobe or (as shown in the second part of this presentation) Toyota and Microsoft.

Valuation Methodologies

If investors are to use a bottom-up process to focus on individual companies, they will have to make cross-border and cross-industry comparisons every day. A vital provision is to avoid comparing apples to oranges. This section examines three of the new but relatively complex approaches to solving this problem—EVA (economic value added), SVA (shareholder value added), and CFROI (cash flow return on investment). Although a substantial body of academic and accounting opinion highlights the inadequacies of the traditional measures, these measures remain the basic tools of almost all practitioners. Only enterprise value (market capitalization plus net debt) to earnings before interest, taxes, depreciation, and amortization, which has the horrible acronym of EV/EBITDA, has gained a wide usage.

Figure 2. Opportunities Available by Country or Sector: Japan and Germany

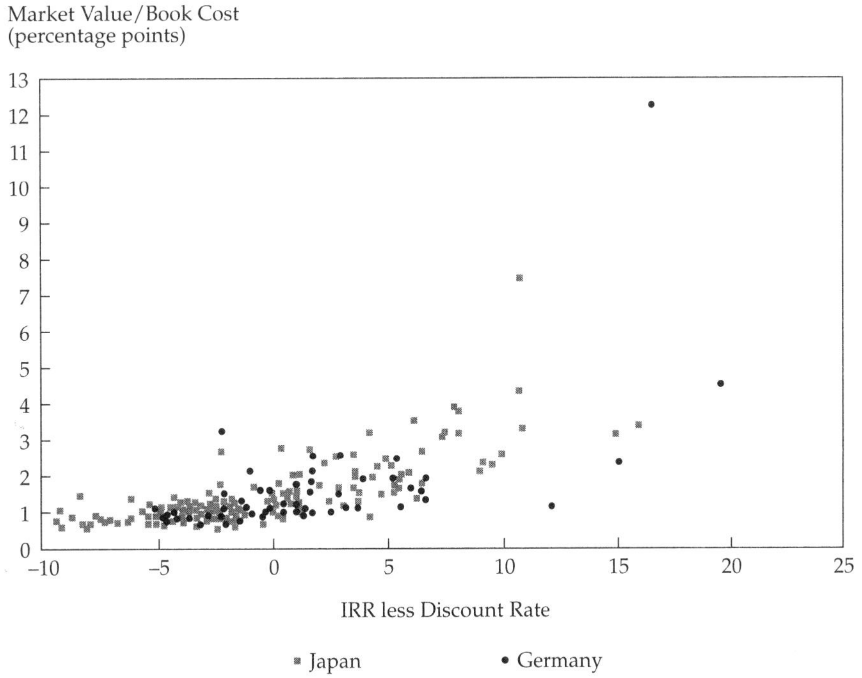

Source: Based on data from HOLT Value Associates

Figure 3. Performance Comparison of Auto and Technology Industries

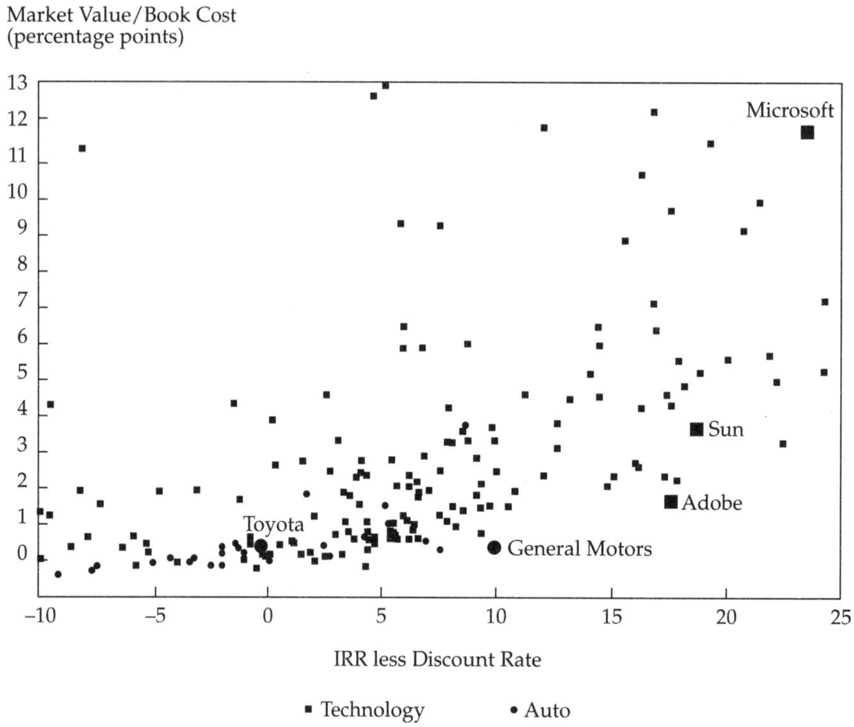

Source: Based on data from HOLT Value Associates

Traditional Methods. Three traditional valuation measures are P/E, EV/EBITDA, and ROI (return on investment). Among these measures, the most popular approach is still P/E, the principal driver of which is earnings per share. Unfortunately, establishing a clear connection between EPS growth and shareholder return is difficult. In fact, in the United States, the inverse correlation has held over the past 12 years. In addition, EPS has two principal weaknesses. First, because it takes no account of fixed- and working-capital requirements, it fails to consider the investment required to generate earnings. Second, EPS ignores the time value of money—the basic requirement that investments should achieve a return above the relevant cost of capital. Of course, returns below the cost of capital destroy value.

In order to address these two concerns, some analysts now use EV/EBITDA, which is merely a glorified P/E. Warren Buffett has described this measure as "utter nonsense" because any business with substantial fixed assets will need to reinvest cash simply to stay in the same place. Analysts most often apply EV/EBITDA to global telecommunications companies and other capital-intensive businesses in order to make them appear more attractive as investments.

A focus on the depreciation policies of the global telecommunications companies further highlights the folly of EV/EBITDA. A correlation apparently exists between return on capital and the speed of depreciation of fixed assets, although one would expect only modest differences in depreciation between comparable businesses. The accounting rules governing depreciation are broadly the same in most counties; the differences are mostly the result of management choice. The implication is that companies choose depreciation policies based more on how they affect net income than their relationship with the underlying asset's economic life.

Measures of ROI are helpful in valuation but still rely on earnings per share. The denominator, book value, is also subject to accounting policies on depreciation and the capitalization of expenses and often includes undepreciated assets of businesses unrelated to the current earnings stream.

The simple example used by Rappaport (1986), a restaurant that requires an initial investment of US$1 million and has a five-year life span, as shown in **Table 1**, reveals the limitations of ROI. The ROI calculation varies substantially year by year and averages 23 percent over the life of the asset, but the economic return on investment—using a discounted cash flow—is 15 percent in each year. In other words, if the cost of capital was 15 percent, the real economic return would be zero.

Table 1. Limitations of ROI: One Restaurant, Inc.

Measure	1999	2000	2001	2002	2003	Total
Return on investment						
Cash flow	$176,230	$250,000	$350,000	$400,000	$400,000	
Depreciation	–200,000	–200,000	–200,000	–200,000	–200,000	
Net income	–23,770	50,000	150,000	200,000	200,000	$ 576,230
Book value (average)	900,000	700,000	500,000	300,000	100,000	2,500,000
ROI	–2.6%	7.1%	30.0%	66.7%	200.0%	23.0%
Economic return on investment						
Cash flow	$ 176,230	$250,000	$350,000	$400,000	$400,000	
PV, beginning	1,000,000	973,755	869,800	650,280	374,840	
PV, end	973,755	869,800	650,280	374,840	0	
Change	–26,245	–106,955	–219,520	–302,440	–347,840	
Economic income	149,985	146,045	130,480	97,560	52,160	
Economic return on investment[a]	15.0%	15.0%	15.0%	15.0%	15.0%	

[a]Economic income/Present value, beginning.

Source: Based on data from CPS Alcar.

Exhibit 1 summarizes the requirements for three traditional valuation methodologies. The traditional measures may be easy to use for basic applications, but they fail to meet most of the requirements of global investors. These measures also are difficult to use in cross-border situations; lack predictive ability; and do not account for risk, incremental investments, or the concept that, over time, returns for all but the most exceptional franchises revert to the mean.

Alternative Methods. An alphabet soup of new valuation methods has sprung up, and EVA, SVA, and CFROI have emerged as the three dominant approaches. Although each of these three methods is a substantial improvement on the traditional methods, each has its own disadvantages. These alternative methods are aimed more at large corporations than at investors and have their origin in the need to establish tools to measure corporate divisional performance for executive compensation schemes. The fund management community has been slow to adopt the methodologies because they are complex and expensive to implement.

Exhibit 1. Comparison of Traditional Valuation Methods

Requirement	P/E	EV/EBITDA	ROI
Simple and easy to use	Y	Y	Y
Applicable across borders and industries	N	N	N
Correlated with total shareholder returns	N	N	?
Accounts for risk	N	N	N
Accounts for incremental investments	N	N	Y
Incorporates mean reversion	N	N	N
Estimates change in value	N	N	N

The concept of value creation is as old as the concept of limited liability. Value arises when an investment creates benefits that exceed costs. Benefits accrue now and in the future, and costs should include the marginal cost of capital. Analysts also have to consider the value of the company after the forecast period and allow for the concept that returns fade up or down over time. General Electric Company made the first systematic attempt to measure value creation in the 1950s. GE used its residual income method, which is the direct antecedent of EVA, to assess its business divisions by calculating each division's net operating profit after taxes (NOPAT) and then subtracting a charge for invested capital.

To illustrate this approach, **Table 2** represents a company with a beginning capital of $4,571 that has NOPAT of $1,100, which grows by $100 each year until 2003. An additional capital expenditure, or incremental investment, of $120 is required in each year until 2003. In the model, a capital charge of 10 percent is deducted from NOPAT to derive residual income, which peaks at $995 in 2003. Next, take the present value (PV) of each year's residual income and assume that the final year's residual income is sustainable in perpetuity. Then, add the cumulative total of present values to the beginning capital to arrive at shareholder value of $13,714.

This analysis has a number of conceptual problems, the most serious of which is that beginning capital has a dramatic effect on residual income in each year. Beginning capital is an accounting estimation of sunk costs and should not be related to forward-looking cash flows. **Table 3** alters the previous example by increasing beginning capital to $13,714, which has the effect of reducing to zero the total cumulative present value of value added. Both companies generate the same NOPAT, but the impact of

Practical Issues in Equity Analysis

Table 2. Residual Income Method

Measure	1999	2000	2001	2002	2003	2004+
NOPAT	$1,100	$1,200	$1,300	$1,400	$1,500	$1,500
Beginning capital	4,571	4,691	4,811	4,831	5,051	5,171
Incremental investment	120	120	120	120	120	0
Capital charge (10 percent)	–457	–469	–481	–493	–505	–517
Residual income	643	731	819	907	995	983
PV of residual income	584	604	615	619	618	6,103
Cumulative PV	584	1,188	1,803	2,422	3,040	9,143
Shareholder value[a]						13,714

[a]Beginning capital plus cumulative PV.
Source: Based on data from CPS Alcar.

Table 3. Influence of Beginning Capital on Residual Income Method

Measure	1999	2000	2001	2002	2003	2004+
NOPAT	$ 1,100	$ 1,200	$ 1,300	$ 1,400	$ 1,500	$ 1,500
Beginning capital	13,714	13,834	13,954	14,074	14,194	14,314
Incremental investment	120	120	120	120	120	0
Capital charge (10 percent)	–1,371	–1,383	–1,395	–1,407	–1,419	–1,431
Residual income	–271	–183	–95	–7	81	69
PV of residual income	–246	–152	–72	–5	50	425
Cumulative PV	–246	–398	–470	–475	–425	0
Shareholder value						13,714

[a]Beginning capital plus cumulative PV.
Source: Based on data from CPS Alcar.

beginning capital on the capital charge would lead management to conclude that the business was destroying value and should be closed or sold.

The residual income approach has three other flaws according to Rappaport. First, the model deducts a noncash charge that is based on the prior year's investment, instead of deducting the actual capital expenditure incurred. Second, NOPAT is the absolute amount in each year and not the change in NOPAT. For example, if the residual income in Year 1 was $643 and no change occurred in NOPAT or investment in succeeding years, the model will add $643 each year. This result occurs despite the fact that the company creates no incremental value. Finally, capitalizing the final year's NOPAT assumes that this level is sustainable in the future.

Residual income is more appropriate for its original intended use as a divisional management accounting tool than in determining shareholder value. Unfortunately, EVA is an evolved form of residual income and suffers from the same defects. EVA uses economic book value instead of beginning capital, and NOPAT is adjusted for what are called "equity equivalents," which are principally deferred taxes, goodwill, LIFO reserves, and cumulative writedowns. As with residual value, the amount of beginning capital will determine the future EVA in each year. Economic book value is still an accounting approximation of sunk costs.

An investor's return should be measured in terms of the current market value of the business, not initial book value. EVA requires too many adjustments, some of which are controversial. It is also highly sensitive to changes in the cost of capital, which is derived using the capital asset pricing model (CAPM).

The best model of incremental business value is called SVA. Shareholder value is measured by taking the present value of the cash flow from operations over the forecast period, adding the residual value of the business (assuming that it adds no value after the forecast period), and subtracting net debt. Cash flow is simply defined as "cash in," or the increase in sales multiplied by the operating profit margin less taxes and the incremental fixed- and working-capital requirements. The shareholder value is then compared with the current market capitalization to determine the forecast return to shareholders.

The CFROI model is the only model derived by a consulting company that attempts to forecast share prices. This approach is based on the concept of a corporate internal rate of return. A company makes investments that are adjusted for historical inflation—which generates a gross cash flow (depreciation is added back) over a fixed period, or project life. The company receives undepreciated assets (e.g., cash) at the end. Investors need only solve for the internal rate of return and compare this value with a discount rate to see if a company is adding or subtracting value. The model makes a series of adjustments and assumptions in order to give all companies a level playing field.

Companies with positive discount rate spreads should focus on growing assets. Companies with negative spreads should do the opposite by contracting assets and, along with neutral spread companies, focusing on improving CFROIs. This model does not rely on the CAPM but derives its discount rate every month from the market by deriving the rate from the aggregate of market CFROI forecasts and aggregate market value of debt and equity. The rate has varied by country, averaging about 6 percent in the United States and 4 percent in Japan over the past 10 years. The 1998 numbers are 9 percent for the United States and 3 percent for Japan.

Built into the CFROI model is the concept of fade—that is, competition causes CFROI and asset growth rates to regress to the mean over time. The most significant changes in stock prices are normally caused by positive or negative surprises relative to expectations of fade. The CFROI model allows users to customize the fade assumptions.

Exhibit 2 provides a scorecard of the three alternative valuation methodologies. All three methods account for risk and are complex to use. Because SVA and CFROI have positive attributes not shared by EVA, EVA receives the lowest marks among the three methods.

Exhibit 2. Comparison of Three Alternative Valuation Methods

Requirement	EVA	SVA	CFROI
Simple and easy to use	N	?	N
Applicable across borders and industries	N	Y	Y
Correlated with total shareholder returns	N	?	Y
Accounts for risk	Y	Y	Y
Accounts for incremental investments	N	Y	Y
Incorporates mean reversion	N	Y	Y
Estimates change in value	N	Y	Y

Comparing the Methods. Focusing on the two strongest valuation methods, SVA and CFROI, this section compares Toyota and Microsoft to determine their future shareholder returns. The capitalization of Microsoft is nearly four times that of Toyota, but Microsoft has only one-fifth of Toyota's sales. As shown in **Table 4**, investors are currently prepared to pay 70 times earnings for Microsoft's nearly 30 percent growth rate and returns. Toyota has altogether more-modest numbers, as would be expected from an auto company. Which company is the better investment today?

Table 4. Traditional Measures: Toyota versus Microsoft

Measure	Toyota	Microsoft
Market capitalization	$100 billion	$375 billion
EPS growth	2%	29%
P/E	27	70
ROE	6.3%	27%
Market-to-book ratio	1.94	22.48
EV/EBITDA	7.6	44.6

Table 5. Assumptions for SVA Analysis: Toyota versus Toyota

Measure	Toyota	Microsoft
Sales in base year (March 1999)	$104 billion	$18 billion
Five-year sales growth rate	3%	25%
Average operating profit margin	5.7	45
Cash tax rate	45	30
Incremental fixed-capital investment rate	100	0
Incremental working-capital investment rate	50	–30

■ *SVA.* The SVA model has six factors—sales growth, operating profit margin, cash income tax rate, incremental working-capital investment rate, incremental fixed-capital investment rate, and cost of capital.

The assumptions shown in **Table 5** for Toyota and Microsoft are based on current margins, tax rates, and sales growth rate forecasts. Table 5 draws on the experience of the past five years to derive the incremental fixed- and working-capital requirements. Note that Toyota spends $1.50 on investments for every incremental sales dollar, whereas Microsoft receives an additional 30 cents.

Toyota's 3 percent sales growth rate and operating margin of 5.7 percent are not enough to generate sufficient cash to cover incremental investments, as shown in the "cash flow from operations" panel of **Table 6**. Over a five-year period, Toyota will destroy more than US$700 million in value at current rates of investment.

The next step is to add the cumulative present value of NOPAT to the present value of the residual value, as shown in the "implied return" panel of Table 6. Capitalizing the initial year's NOPAT at the 5 percent cost of capital derives the residual value. The total of the present values of cash flow from operations and residual value is corporate value, from which net debt is subtracted.

As Toyota destroys value, shareholder value declines in each year. By dividing shareholder value by the number of outstanding shares, investors can compare the implied future share price with the current price of ¥3,000 and calculate the implied annual compound return to shareholders. At current

©2000, Association for Investment Management and Research 71

Table 6. SVA Analysis: Toyota
(US$ in millions)

Measure	1999	2000	2001	2002	2003	2004
Cash flow from operations						
Operating profit	$712	$734	$756	$779	$802	$826
NOPAT	392	404	416	428	441	454
Capital expenditures, depreciation	—	–375	–386	–398	–410	–422
Working capital	—	–187	–193	–199	–205	–211
Cash flow from operations	—	–158	–163	–169	–174	–179
PV at 5 percent	—	–151	–149	–145	–143	–140
Cumulative PV	—	–151	–300	–445	–588	–728
Implied return						
Cumulative PV	—	–$151	$300	–$445	–$588	–$728
Residual value[a]	$7,837	8,073	8,315	8,564	8,821	9,085
PV of residual value	7,837	7,688	7,541	7,398	7,257	7,118
Total value	$7,837	$7,536	$7,242	$6,953	$6,669	$6,391
Net debt	–2,539	–2,539	–2,539	–2,539	–2,359	–2,539
Shareholder value	$5,298	$4,997	$4,703	$4,114	$4,130	$3,852
Per share[b]	1,398	1,320	1,241	1,164	1,090	1,016
Implied return (current price ¥3,000)	—	–56%	–36%	–27%	–22%	–19%

[a]Residual value capitalizes NOPAT in each year at the cost of capital and assumes that depreciation covers maintenance capital expenditures and working capital.
[b]Actual dollar amounts, not in millions.

---

rates of sales growth, margins, and incremental investment, Toyota will have a negative net worth by 2021. The company needs to double operating margins to a "threshold margin" of 13 percent to add shareholder value, at which point Toyota will be worth ¥4,000 per share.

At ¥3,000 per share, the assumed margin improvement is from the current forecast of 5.7 percent to 10.5 percent. Higher bond yields will raise the cost of capital and the threshold margin. An increase to 6 percent would require operating margins of 15.4 percent in order to add value. If no improvement occurs, the 1999 fair value of Toyota is ¥1,000 per share, which is equal to a zero return on an investment in the company for five years from today. This analysis has not allowed for the value of investments that are not core to the business, such as land or cross-holding of shares, that could be sold or realized and deducted from net debt. In Toyota's case, these noncore investments may add as much as ¥1,000 per share.

In contrast, Microsoft is a value creator. As shown by the cumulative present value for the "cash flow from operations" panel in **Table 7**, Microsoft adds nearly $50 billion over the next five years, given a 10 percent cost of capital. In this projection, shareholder value in 2004 would total US$167 billion. Unfortunately, the "implied return" panel of Table 7 indicates that this amount is only 44 percent of current market capitalization.

Subtracting the base-year value of nearly $69 billion, Microsoft shareholders are anticipating an additional $306 billion in value added. Shareholder returns will exceed the cost of capital only if the company can sustain growth and returns at or above the current levels for at least 10 years. Alternatively, if the value growth duration for Microsoft is only five years, after which it produces returns only in line with the cost of capital, the estimated fair value is nearly $67 per share, implying a five-year return of –15 percent.

SVA has its problems. For example, SVA accepts the CAPM. Users must tailor the model to each company, so SVA is more useful in corporate forecasting than investing. In the current analysis, SVA seems to be divorced from market realities—Toyota's share price tripled while value was destroyed because the market thought that the weaker yen had improved the company's pricing power.

SVA also does not help with the sell decision. For the average fund manager, using SVA to determine Microsoft's value growth duration is not easy. Finally, the residual value is sensitive to NOPAT in the base year.

■ *CFROI.* Toyota's shares were clearly undervalued in the late 1980s. Export stocks were out of favor, and the company was underinvesting in its business. Unlike Honda, Toyota failed to go global at this time. Because the automobile business has

Table 7. SVA Analysis: Microsoft
(US$ in billions)

Measure	1999	2000	2001	2002	2003	2004
Cash flow from operations						
Operating profit	$7.88	$9.84	$12.30	$15.68	$19.23	$24.03
NOPAT	5.51	6.89	8.61	10.77	13.46	16.82
Capital expenditures, depreciation	—	0	0	0	0	0
Working capital	—	1.31	1.64	2.05	2.56	3.20
Cash flow from operations	—	8.20	10.25	12.82	16.02	20.03
PV at 10 percent	—	7.46	8.47	9.63	10.94	12.44
Cumulative PV	—	7.46	15.93	25.56	36.50	48.94
Implied return						
Cumulative PV	—	$ 7.46	$15.93	$ 25.56	$ 36.50	$ 48.94
Residual value	$55.13	68.91	86.13	107.67	134.58	168.23
PV of residual value	55.13	62.64	71.18	80.89	91.92	104.46
Total value	$55.13	$70.10	$87.12	$106.45	$128.43	$153.40
Less net debt	13.70	13.70	13.70	13.70	13.70	13.70
Shareholder value	$68.83	$83.80	$100.82	$120.15	$142.13	$167.10
Per share[a]	27.53	33.52	40.33	48.06	56.85	66.84
Implied return (current price $150)	—	–77%	–48%	–32%	–21%	–15%

[a] Actual dollar amounts, not in millions

become more competitive and domestic margins have been squeezed, Toyota now has a negative spread, but at the same time, its investment spending has risen dramatically.

In 1998 and 1999, the market has welcomed Toyota's belated globalization and expects the company to benefit from the weakness of the yen, but the model predicts future underperformance.

The final step is to relate the analysis to future share price performance. CFROI, asset growth, and fade are combined in this model to create future net cash receipts, which are influenced by corporate value drivers and decisions. Net cash receipts are then discounted at a rate based on the market discount rate adjusted for company size and leverage to arrive at a future price. The expected price ranges can then be graphed and compared with the actual results.

Today, the target, or best price, is 10 percent below the current price levels, and the worst-case valuation is ¥2,171. The deviation of forecast from the actual is a relatively high 29, with zero being perfectly correlated, but the model has been mostly right during the 1990s and suggests moderate underperformance in the future.

Microsoft's CFROI has been very high but cyclical. Asset growth has rightly been very high, but the model forecasts that both will decline, suggesting potential stock price weakness. The best price is $92, and the worst price is $57, which is close to the SVA model's five-year value growth duration. The company is ranked in the ninth decile in terms of future share price performance. The historical accuracy of the model is very high.

CFROI also has its problems. The market-specific discount rate does not make allowance for industry factors or for global companies to which blended discount rates should be applied. Project life is estimated from depreciation or a weighted average, based on asset composition, and is subject to the vagaries of depreciation policies.

Outside the United States, the fade calculation is automatic. In the United States, a better approach is to adopt company-specific fade rates, using past volatility and levels of reinvestment to forecast a five-year fade. The model also does not work well in certain industries. In particular, property, leasing, and exploration are areas in which estimating project life is often difficult. Finally, the model is not easy to replicate and is very expensive for those who use the service.

Summary. Of the three methods reviewed, CFROI gets the highest marks and, for those investment companies willing to pay the price, is the best solution. At Dresdner Asset Management, we have found that imposing a new tool on fund managers takes patience. The CFROI, however, was put to good use during the October 1998 decline in world equity markets. We were able to identify which stocks were vulnerable to deterioration in market sentiment and which stocks did not have sufficient cash flow backing to justify their current market capitalization. For the most part, CFROI confirmed why certain stocks were worth holding, and those stocks' subsequent performance has borne out this analysis.

All of these methods are only tools that depend on inputs and subjective evaluation. Investors should first focus on the two most important drivers of future returns—business and management. If one of the new methods is to prevail, the lead must come from the fund management community. Some leading companies are now devoting considerable resources to improving their valuation methodologies. The test is whether the additional effort enhances alpha, and to date, the case is, to adopt a Scottish legal verdict, not proven.

Conclusion

As investors globalize and focus more on sectors than on countries, P/E and other traditional measures become less helpful. Fund management companies can add value to the investment process by incorporating some of the techniques from the new valuation models, which have become an increasingly important part of managers' ability to generate excess return for clients.

Introducing new valuation methodologies requires a firmwide re-education and works best if it is first offered as an alternative and additional tool. The investment process should start with identifying great businesses run by competent people motivated to maintain high rates of return on future investments. Only after these criteria have been met should investors begin to consider valuation.

Valuing Zero-Income Stocks: A Practical Approach

Barney Wilson
Vice President and Equity Research Analyst
Putnam Investments

> The emergence of Internet-related companies has led to a dramatic increase in the number of zero-income stocks, and exposure to these stocks is becoming increasingly unavoidable. Unfortunately for analysts trying to perform valuations, the peculiar nature of these companies poses unusual pitfalls. Several key adjustments to the traditional present-value approach are necessary to avoid critical errors in the valuation process.

The high-growth/high-risk stocks of zero-income companies, most notably Internet-related companies, are entering the investing mainstream. Given the increasing exposure to such stocks through benchmarks and indexes, investors have to come to terms with this type of stock if only to avoid making costly errors. Developing a meaningful view on these companies means adopting a new attitude toward valuation, one that emphasizes probability over potentially misleading precision. The key is to make appropriate adjustments to the traditional present-value method.

This presentation has three goals: to highlight the increasing importance of having a view on how to value zero-income stocks, to identify the primary areas of difficulty in applying a traditional present-value methodology to these stocks, and to offer some adjustments to a traditional present-value methodology that will improve the model's effectiveness for the valuation of such companies.

The Importance of Having a View

The real driver behind the increasing importance of zero-income or low-earnings stocks is the emergence of the Internet. As a result, more midcap and large-cap stocks without earnings are appearing in the benchmarks and universes of midcap and large-cap growth funds. The valuation challenge posed by these stocks, therefore, is no longer one faced only by small-cap managers. The challenge is particularly difficult for large-cap managers because they are not as comfortable with such volatile stocks as small-cap managers are. All serious investors must confront the issue and develop a way of valuing this type of high-growth/high-risk stock.

Companies with little or no earnings but large market capitalizations are becoming increasingly common, which has important implications. **Figure 1** charts the universe of U.S. public companies with market caps greater than $100 million and sorts them by the ratio of market cap to 12-month trailing revenue. The vast majority of the companies have market cap/trailing revenue of less than 2.5. Of the 255 companies in this universe that have a ratio greater than 10, 119 have a ratio greater than 20, and companies with even greater ratios exist. The market caps for these companies tend to change significantly on a day-to-day basis. As of December 1998, Amazon.com had a market cap of $11 billion and Yahoo! had a market cap of $23 billion. Both stocks had had phenomenal year-to-date performances—more than 800 percent for Amazon and more than 600 percent for Yahoo!. A couple of years ago, a fund manager could say these two stocks were too risky and not even look at them, but such stocks now appear in important indexes. Amazon and Yahoo! now account for 2.5 percent of the Russell Midcap Growth Index, an index against which client money is benchmarked. Managers can no longer simply ignore such stocks—because they have exposure to *not* owning them.

The other significant reason for having a view on these stocks is to avoid becoming confused about the strange things that have been happening. For example, the eBay initial public offering had a filing range of $14–$16 in September 1998. On the first day of trading, the price went up to $54, and it hit $84 on November 2. Then, one of the sell-side analysts

Figure 1. Ratio of Market Cap to Trailing Revenue, October 1998
(companies with market caps greater than $100 million)

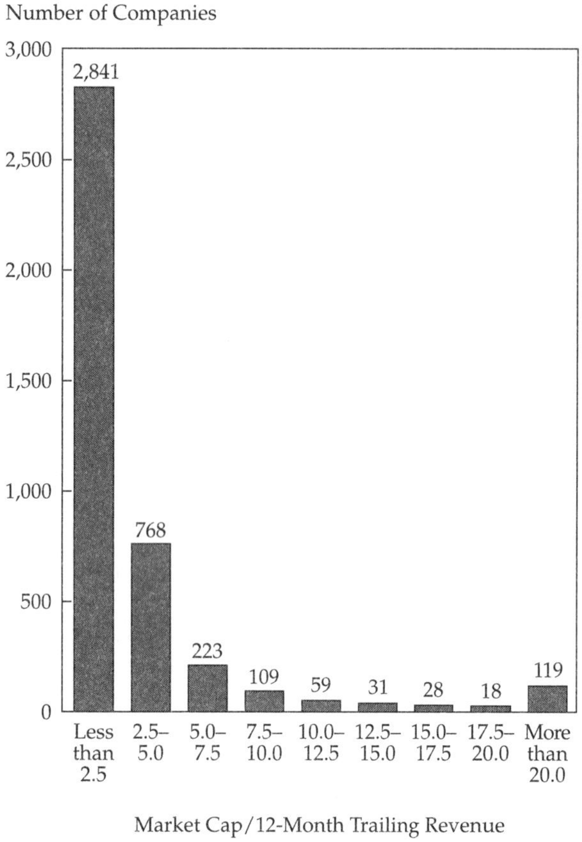

Number of Companies

Market Cap/12-Month Trailing Revenue	Number of Companies
Less than 2.5	2,841
2.5–5.0	768
5.0–7.5	223
7.5–10.0	109
10.0–12.5	59
12.5–15.0	31
15.0–17.5	28
17.5–20.0	18
More than 20.0	119

Source: Based on data from Baseline.

increased the target price to $150—which was 50 times projected 1999 revenues. The stock hit a high of $218 on November 27. Another peculiar example is the sell-side analyst from one of the top 10 investment banks who came into our office and said that even though he could not justify Amazon's valuation, we should buy the stock simply because it was going up. Sell-side analysts have had buy ratings on stocks trading at twice their target price. With such attitudes becoming more common, investors need a discipline for reaching their own conclusions about the value of stocks with little or no earnings.

The solution, however, is not so simple as deciding to have a view. Developing a view is a challenge in itself because the uncertainty of these stocks hinders the effectiveness of the traditional present-value methodology. In fact, using the same approach for high-growth/high-risk stocks as for more typical companies can produce results that are completely misleading. In order to get a more realistic valuation, investors must understand the shortcomings of the standard approach and make a variety of modifications.

Problems with Traditional Present-Value Methodology

The primary valuation methodology we use in Putnam's Equity Research department is based on a traditional present-value approach. The concept is very logical to us because we believe the value of a stock is at its core the value of its discounted cash flows. Also, the approach avoids accounting distortions and is not dependent on comparable-company valuations, which is an important feature. Because valuations of Internet stocks fluctuate so much, the less use of comparables, the better. In addition, the present-value method factors in risk, incorporates future investment needs, and allows analysts to look at return on capital, which we believe is critically important.

For application to high-growth/high-risk stocks, however, the present-value method has three main problems: determining a reasonable range for critical variables, setting the discount rate, and establishing the fade rate.

Wide Range of Critical Variables. The critical variables in the present-value method—revenue growth, margins, working capital, capital expenditures, and returns—can have a very wide range for an Internet-type stock.

Consider the example of revenue growth. In forecasting the revenues of a traditional company, analysts predict revenues two years out. They take a base case—for, say, a beverage company—and then add/subtract 3 percent. For many companies, analysts can be confident that the value will be within, or at least close to, this range. For example, in fall 1996, Anheuser-Busch's revenue estimate for two years out was $11.4 billion, and as of December 1998, Anheuser-Busch had $11.1 billion in revenue—not far off the estimate.

Basic probability distributions demonstrate how uncertainty varies among different types of companies. **Figure 2** illustrates the normal probability distribution, the familiar bell-shaped curve with the peak of the bell representing both the weighted average of the possible outcomes and the highest probability case and the tails representing highly unlikely outcomes. For a traditional low-risk company, the probability of actual revenues being within plus or minus 3 percent of forecast is high—about 60–70 percent. Obviously, the lowest-risk kind of company has the narrowest distribution. As distance from the base case increases, however, the probability of the outcome decreases. For a medium-risk company, the bell becomes a little wider.

Figure 2. Probability Distributions for Traditional Companies with Three Levels of Risk

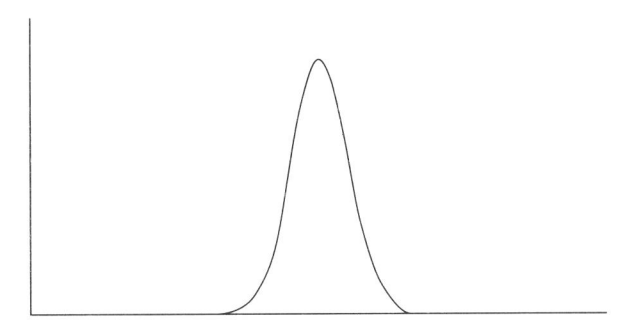

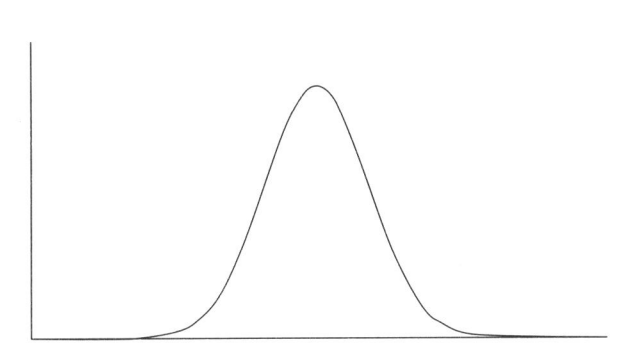

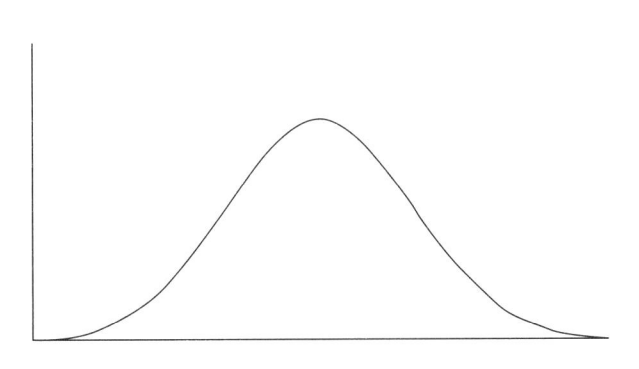

Even the potential revenue growth of the higher-risk *traditional* companies (such as an established technology company) is still represented by a normal distribution. A traditional company with relatively high risk will simply have a much wider bell of probability and, therefore, greater uncertainty of an accurate forecast. The result is still a normal distribution, with the highest probability case in the center and the tails thin.

The previous examples are in stark contrast to high-growth/high-risk companies. In trying to forecast what an Internet company's revenues will be a couple of years out, analysts still must begin with a base case, but such companies have an extremely wide range of possible revenues—perhaps as much as 50 percent higher or 50 percent lower than forecast (and even that range may not be a wide enough).

Consider the example of Connect, a technology stock associated with the Internet. In fall 1996, the two-year revenue estimate was $51 million. As of December 1998, that company had about $6 million in revenues, 88 percent less than the original estimate.

Yahoo! is a positive example of the extent to which the actual outcome may differ from the estimate. In fall 1996, the company's revenue estimate for calendar 1998 was $60 million. As of December 1998, Yahoo! had about $190 million in revenue for the year, so the actual revenues exceeded the original estimate by more than 200 percent.

Whether the result is good or bad, the important point is that the actual revenues of a high-growth/high-risk company are unlikely to be close to the base-case forecast. Consider the example of a company that, in November 1998, had projected total 1998 revenue of about $8 million. The sell-side analyst behind the company's IPO was projecting $55 million in revenue a few years out, but in reality, the company is unlikely to come within a couple million dollars of $55 million in revenue. It almost certainly will be either significantly above or below the estimate. As **Figure 3** shows, Internet-type stocks have a bimodal distribution—either extremely successful or extremely unsuccessful. So, high-growth/high-risk companies have a nonnormal probability distribution, which is another way of stating the basic problem: For such companies, the present-value method requires an extremely wide range for the critical variables.

Discount Rate. The second difficulty in valuing these companies is getting the right discount rate. At Putnam, we build up to our discount rate by starting with a risk-free rate and adding a market risk premium and a company-specific risk premium. For the company-specific risk premium, the range is typically between +1 percentage point and –1 percentage point. So, for simplicity, for the S&P 500 company of average risk, assume a 10 percent discount rate; for lower risk, a 9 percent discount rate; and for higher risk, an 11 percent discount rate.

To increase this 11 percent discount rate to 15 or 16 percent simply because the Internet company is extremely risky is not the solution. Using this approach and acting on it could cause you to lose large amounts of money, as you could both sell appreciating stocks too early and buy declining

Figure 3. Nonnormal Probability Distribution for a High-Growth/High-Risk Company

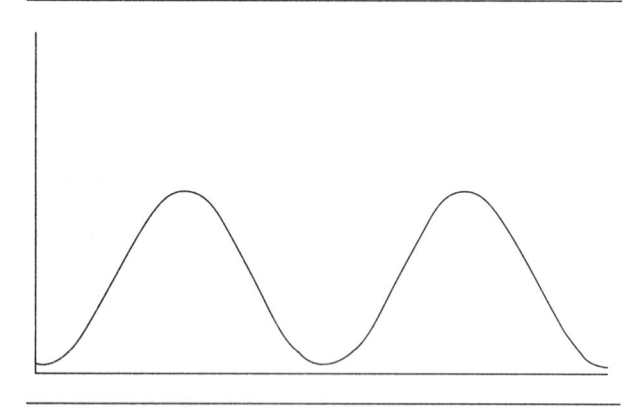

stocks too early. The bell curve for the discount rate widens as the company in question gets slightly more risky. Although this approach is well suited to traditional companies, for companies with a nonnormal distribution, such as the Internet companies, the framework breaks down. Simply increasing the discount rate by a few percentage points cannot account for the extraordinary increase in uncertainty that results from the bimodal distribution typical of high-growth/high-risk companies.

Fade Rate. The third difficulty involves the fade rate, the rate at which the growth of a company converges on its default terminal growth rate. In our present-value models at Putnam, the fade rate for a traditional company gets relatively little attention because the valuation is typically not very sensitive to this variable. For the high-growth/high-risk companies, however, the valuation is extremely sensitive to the variable, which makes determining the right fade critical. To analyze Amazon.com, for example, and forecast that it will grow 100 percent for three or four years and then have a 40 percent growth rate for five years is challenging enough, but to have conviction as to how that 40 percent fades down to a terminal growth rate of 4 or 5 percent is even more challenging.

Variations in fade rate can have enormous implications, which makes sensitivity analysis crucial. **Table 1** shows a sensitivity analysis on the fade rate that compares a high-growth/high-risk company with a traditional company. The base case is a 10 percent fade rate, for which the fair value is normalized to 100 for both hypothetical companies. If the fade rate is increased to 12 percent, the fade happens more quickly, reducing value. If it is decreased, the fade happens more slowly and increases value. For the high-growth/high-risk company, if the fade rate is lowered to 8 percent and then 6 percent, the value of the company increases sixfold. In contrast, for the traditional company, the value of the company increases only 25 percent. The fade rate, which is merely in the background for the valuation of traditional companies, becomes an important consideration in valuing high-growth/high-risk companies.

Table 1. Sensitivity Analysis of Fade Rate for a High-Growth/High-Risk Company and a Traditional Company

Company Type	6%	8%	10%	12%	14%
High-growth/high-risk company					
Fair value	602	205	100	60	41
Traditional company					
Fair value	125	110	100	93	88

Summary. Using an unmodified version of a traditional present-value method for the valuation of high-growth/high-risk stocks is almost futile. The combined uncertainties of the critical variables, the discount rate, and the fade rate simply overwhelm the standard framework and render it meaningless. Investors, however, do not have the luxury of ignoring such stocks. Fortunately, a straightforward modification exists, which we believe provides insight into the value of these stocks.

Adjustments to a Traditional Present-Value Methodology

At Putnam, we make three adjustments to account for the problems with present-value valuation. First, we conceptually distinguish between the hypergrowth period and the subsequent period of traditional growth. Second, we use scenario analysis. Finally, we supplement our discounted cash flow (DCF) analysis, or present-value approach, with other tools.

Distinguishing between Growth Periods. Distinguishing between the hypergrowth period and the subsequent period of traditional growth is crucial. Making this distinction allows for the use of different discount rates for different periods, facilitates scenario analysis, and reduces the importance of the fade rate.

Scenario Analysis. After doing the DCF analysis for the upside case, the base case, and the downside case, the analyst will have a fair value for each case, as shown in the following example for a hypothetical company:

Case	Expected Value	Probability of Happening
Upside case	$48	60%
Base case	15	20
Downside case	1	20

Note that the fair value for the downside case of many Internet stocks can be a dollar or less per share, because the unsuccessful companies will never generate meaningful cash flow.

The next step is to assign a probability to each of the scenarios. Preferably, the base case should not be the highest probability case because the bimodal distribution typical of these companies indicates that the base case is less likely to occur than more-extreme outcomes. For most Internet companies, the future is boom or bust, not something in between.

Some would say that the next logical step is to interpret the probability-adjusted expected value to mean that the expected value, or fair value, of the stock is the weighted average. This view, however, is not meaningful. What does have meaning is focusing on the probabilities and the expected values related to these stocks.

If the stock were trading at the expected value, an investor would conclude that the stock is not an interesting investment because it has such a high degree of risk. Using the same information and thinking in terms of probabilities would indicate a 60 percent chance that the upside scenario will come to pass. Probability is the right place for the analyst to focus because the analysis concentrates on *why* the upside case has a 60 percent chance of occurring. This is where the framework is useful in making action-oriented decisions—if, for example, at the end of the analysis, there is a 60 percent or greater chance of the upside case coming to pass and the fair value of the upside case is substantially above the current price, we are likely to buy the stock.

Using the adjusted DCF approach with scenario analysis is an effective method because it avoids the problems with determining the discount rate and the fade rate. This method also gets away from taking the average of disparate possible outcomes.

The DCF method focuses the analyst's attention on the probabilities and magnitudes, which reduces the false impression of precision. The approach is also flexible enough to be useful. Without a flexible approach, an analyst trying to value high-growth/high-risk stocks runs the risk of finding the analysis framework to be too rigid and then taking a more speculative approach to valuation.

Our approach is very useful in interpreting breaking news or sharply moving stock prices. For example, news reports about Internet stocks often suggest that the upside case will not result in more cash coming to the company, but the same report may also indicate that the probability of the upside case coming to pass has increased. This framework allows investors to interpret that information.

Supplements to DCF Analysis. When evaluating zero-income stocks, investors may supplement the DCF model with other analytical tools. The most common supplements are the price-to-sales ratio (P/S), certain applications of the price-to-earnings ratio (P/E), evaluation of the 52-week high/low price, and a market-cap "reality check." Some of these supplements have merit; some do not.

■ *Price-to-sales ratio.* One of the most common tools used by sell-side analysts is P/S analysis. At Putnam, we do not consider this information meaningful for Internet-type stocks. For a P/S far from the average P/S of the S&P 500 Index or the average-growth company, the numbers quickly lose meaning—a P/S of 56.8 does not hold any significance.

■ *Price-to-earnings ratio.* Although many believers in present-value approaches have nearly complete disdain for looking at P/E, our view is that, although looking at P/E has many negatives, in certain circumstances a meaningful correlation exists between a relatively clean P/E and a DCF valuation. Without getting bogged down in the details, the correlation has the most meaning when the P/E is reasonably close to the market P/E. The correlation breaks down and loses meaning when the P/E is at levels of twice the market P/E or more. To give a rough example of where the correlation holds, if an established growth company has a growth rate somewhat above the market, a cash return on capital somewhat above the market, and reasonable margin, I have confidence that a DCF "fair value" will correspond to a P/E above that of the market but probably not twice that of the market. An example of a case in which the correlation does not hold is a company growing at 100 percent off a small revenue base and experiencing margin expansion—a well-done DCF could correspond to a P/E off next year's earnings of 50 or of 250, depending on the situation. Thus, looking at P/E is useless in this case.

Because of the way we think about P/Es, we do not find the approach of looking to other high-P/E companies as "comps" to be useful in understanding the value of a high-growth company. We have had many sell-side analysts argue that XYZ company "deserves" an 80 P/E off of next year's earnings for two reasons: Its growth rate is 80 percent, and similar companies are trading at an average P/E of 80. Because we believe there is little correlation between an 80 P/E and a cash-flow-based valuation, we find unpersuasive these arguments for using "comparable P/Es" to value high-growth companies.

Also, because we do find there to be a correlation between reasonable P/Es and DCF valuations, we do at times use a short-cut or abbreviated version of our adjusted DCF with scenario analysis when valuing high-growth companies. The abbreviated form of the adjusted DCF with scenario analysis involves taking a P/E to get the dollar value at the end of the hypergrowth period, rather than doing DCF valuation at the end of the hypergrowth period. This abbreviated method requires the use of a P/E based on "real" earnings—that is, adjusted for amortization or anything else that would cause the earnings to differ substantially from the cash flow. Then, the analyst simply discounts back to the present at the required rate of return.

This abbreviated approach has all the flaws of P/E analysis, but it has certain advantages. It is a simple and accessible approach. P/Es have some correlation to DCF values, and much of the market looks at P/Es. Also, using P/E to evaluate a particular company is quicker than using a DCF approach.

■ *The 52-week high/low.* The next possible supplement in valuing these high-growth/high-risk stocks is to consider how far the current price is above/below the 52-week high/low price, a measurement used by almost all sell-side analysts. This supplement, however, is not useful. It attributes meaning to the spikes and dips in the stock price, even though the short-term stock price is a function of supply/demand for the stock, not a function of the value of the company.

■ *Market-cap reality check.* Investors should also consider making market-cap reality checks. As Internet-type stocks start to increase in valuation, market capitalizations may equal or exceed some of the real-world companies. Although Yahoo! and America Online are sometimes referred to as media-type companies, their market caps are higher than such media giants as News Corporation or CBS Corporation. This observation does not automatically mean that Yahoo! and AOL are overvalued. An investor thinking about purchasing AOL or Yahoo! needs to have a view as to why the market cap is significantly higher than that of the existing major players in the media world.

In addition, other logical reality checks can be helpful. For example, obviously, investors would want to be sure that they are not projecting that a company's revenues will exceed the size of its particular market.

Conclusion

The increasing prominence of low-earnings companies in the market leaves little room for serious investors to avoid exposure to such stocks. Minimizing the risk of potentially costly errors in the valuation of these stocks, however, requires not merely adjustments of technique but a change of focus. The keys are understanding that multiple scenarios exist, learning to focus on the probabilities and magnitudes associated with each scenario, and avoiding being tied to a single "fair value" for a stock.

Question and Answer Session

Barney Wilson

Question: Are Internet-type stocks easily influenced by buying and selling, especially by individual investors who don't even have a sense of valuation?

Wilson: Very much so. For many of these stocks, especially the smaller-cap stocks, a complete disconnect occurs between the value of the stock and the value of the company, with the value of the stock being determined in some cases by a lot of day traders and retail individual traders who aren't looking at the value of the company.

For example, eBay's IPO in September 1998 sold 3.5 million shares. The average daily volume on Nasdaq at that time was around 3 million shares a day. If you take half of that amount because of double counting on Nasdaq, about half of the outstanding shares of eBay trade hands every day. The fact is that the investors who are buying those stocks do not think these are undervalued shares. Instead, they are people who are day trading and trying to make a quick profit, so they are not necessarily worried about the value of the company. Benjamin Graham observed that in the short run the stock market is a voting machine and in the long run it's a weighing machine. Over longer periods of time, whether 6 months, a year, or 18 months, these stock prices will correlate with the value of the companies and the companies' ability to produce revenue growth, earnings growth, and cash flow growth. In the short term, the stock price is simply determined by supply and demand for the stock without regard for the value of the company.

Question: Are qualitative considerations—such as evaluating the competence of management—important for the valuation of Internet-type stocks?

Wilson: For these stocks, management is extremely important, and it is one of the qualitative factors we evaluate, not only in terms of whether the management is good but also in terms of the management's history, track record, and vision. AOL, for example, has differentiated management. Bob Pittman, AOL's president and chief operating officer, is an outstanding brand manager and has a proven track record of making media ventures work—he was behind MTV and Six Flags Theme Parks. AOL is an example of management that is differentiated. Many of these Internet-type companies have management with more technology-related backgrounds. The management team is extremely important because the Internet landscape is changing so fast and because much of the game is taking your assets, figuring out how they are valuable, and attaining that value as the business environment continues to change.

Question: Is the market potential of a new business concept easily figured out?

Wilson: Determining market potential comes down to the nuts-and-bolts equity research. The key is to look at the size of the market in which the company must compete and the market capitalization of the company relative to this market. Given the size of the book industry and the music industry and given what the Amazon stock price is implying about how quickly and how large Amazon needs to grow, the company needs to expand beyond its core markets to other markets in order to justify its stock prices. An extremely important point is to understand both the size of the market and what the stable business model will look like. For the retail companies on the Internet, as you try to forecast companies' business models for the future, you should be using retail-type margins, but for media companies, such as Yahoo!, a higher margin makes more sense.

Question: What is the best tool to prevent overanxious portfolio managers from impulsively buying a high-growth/high-risk stock simply because it is hot, as opposed to being a solid investment prospect?

Wilson: Almost everything we do comes back to earnings and cash flow. If we don't see how the company can have strong earnings and cash flow within a couple of years, we stay away from the stock. To buy these stocks for other reasons can be tempting.

Investors are usually inclined to buy a stock for one of three reasons. First, they have a view that the value of the stock understates the value of the company and that, over time, the value of the stock will appreciate to match the value of the company. Second, they have a view, without regard to valuation, that someone will buy the stock from them at a higher price. Or third, they are trying simply to neutralize their exposure to the benchmark. Neutralizing the exposure to the benchmark is a portfolio manager's decision that isn't necessarily crazy. The second reason, simply buying a stock without regard to valuation because you think somebody's going to buy it from you at a higher price, is speculation. The danger is that you think you're investing but you're really speculating. So, it comes down to the first and most basic reason: You think the value of the stock understates the value of the company, and value, which for us is cash flows and earnings, boils down to your valuation approach. I wish there were some magic bullet, but the "tool" is a basic commitment to making sure every investment decision is tied to a view of the earnings and cash flow of the company.

Question: Is Putnam using the methods you have described to evaluate traditional companies?

Wilson: The reason the adjustments are so important for high-growth/high-risk stocks is that our traditional valuation methodology breaks down when applied to these stocks. Scenario analysis, for example, is important for Internet stocks because the base case, which may be the average of the possible outcomes, may not be the highest probability event. In short, we do use some scenario analysis for traditional stocks, but the scenario analysis is much more intensive for Internet stocks.

Analyzing Asian Companies

Richard H. Lawrence, Jr., CFA
Managing Director
Overlook Investments Limited

> Total reliance on traditional valuation methods to evaluate Asian companies can be dangerous because of the companies' lack of transparency and inadequate financial disclosures. Fundamental investment principles still apply, but analysts need to look beyond basic accounting data and often earnings projections. Focusing on cash flow, accounting-adjusted earnings, and enterprise value; making repeated company visits; and evaluating management can all help analysts uncover the common ways in which Asian companies destroy value.

Investors enter a different realm of financial analysis when they seek to find economic reality in the earnings of Asian companies. Different standards of accounting and corporate reporting and different business cultures can impair the effectiveness of analytical methods developed for the evaluation of U.S. companies. To succeed, investors must understand that no one model or approach will provide the right answer. The key is to use a combination of methods—from strict quantitative assessment to basic common sense—to avoid the very real chance of being confused or deceived and to increase the probability of perceiving a company's true situation.

This presentation discusses the aspects necessary for sound financial analysis of Asian companies. In particular, the discussion focuses on the tools, disciplines, practices, and experiences of Overlook Investments, an independent fund manager based in Hong Kong. Overlook's example provides general insights that can benefit any investor trying to find superior investment opportunities in Asia.

Fundamental Principles

Financial analysis of Asian companies requires a strong grasp of fundamental principles. Because Benjamin Graham is the founding father of financial analysis, familiarity with his writings is beneficial. In particular, Graham's *The Intelligent Investor* (first published in 1949) and Graham and Dodd's *Security Analysis* (first published in 1934)—although they may seem like outdated books to some—contain critical learning tools and many insights for all analysts and cannot be reread enough. All the analytical approaches described in this presentation have roots in Graham's work.

Graham provides four major lessons. First, analysts should always use common sense in evaluating securities. Second, analysts should focus on the importance of valuation, meaning that they should tie the value of a security to the company's cash flow. Third, analysts should focus on real earnings, not reported earnings, and the historical ability of management and business to produce real earnings. Finally, analysts should consider the issue of margin of safety.

Cohen, Zinbarg, and Zeikel's *Investment Analysis and Portfolio Management* (1973), another seemingly outdated book, also contains many valuable insights for both industry and company analysis. This book outlines important financial ratios in great detail and promotes return on equity as the key barometer for business performance. The book also presents the DuPont model of financial analysis, which isolates the four critical components of ROE:
- profit margins—gross profit margins; operating profit margins; earnings before interest, taxes, depreciation, and amortization (EBITDA); and net margin;
- asset turnover—total asset turnover, fixed asset turnover, accounts receivable turnover, and inventory turnover;
- capital structure—the debt-to-equity ratio and leverage; and
- the tax rate.

This model works well in the United States because similar accounting policies apply for a large market.

For use in the international arena, analysts should be mindful that the DuPont model has at least four weaknesses. First, differences in accounting policies among countries can badly distort the DuPont model results, and investors and analysts alike must understand such differences. Second, the DuPont model does not consider the impact of inflation, which may lead to comparability problems over time. Third, the model fails to consider risk, which can be of a higher order of magnitude in Asian than in U.S securities markets. Finally, the model does not relate to market valuation, so it is standing on its own as an analytical tool.

Accounting Policies

At Overlook Investments, we focus on cash and search the stock markets throughout Asia for companies that generate real cash earnings. Asian companies are adept at manufacturing both assets and reported profits, but many are less successful at creating cash, particularly in adequate proportion to the capital employed. Unfortunately, many Asian companies have relied on dilutive capital raisings to mask their inability to create free cash from operations. Analysts who track real cash earnings can generally discover most accounting problems that a company faces.

At Overlook, we use the phrase "accounting-adjusted numbers." We manually adjust the income statements, cash flow statements, and balance sheets for any distortions that result from inappropriate accounting policies. Specific accounting polices that must be reviewed with extreme care include the exclusion of certain subsidiaries from the consolidated accounts, the implementation of inappropriate depreciation policies, the use of spin-off of subsidiaries to record nonrecurring income and build "cookie jar" reserves, the use of capitalized interest and preoperating expenses to exaggerate profits, the revaluations of assets that distort debt levels, and the timing of recognition of income and expenses.

Cash Flow

Analysts and investors often use the term cash flow too casually. They need to be precise about which cash flow they mean at a particular time. At Overlook, we use five distinct definitions of cash flow: working capital, cash flow as profits, free cash flow, operating free cash flow, and cash flow of corporate structure.

Working-capital cash flow is defined as inventories and receivables minus payables. This type of cash flow represents working capital tied up in the business. Analysts and investors should look for businesses that have negative working capital—that is, payables exceed receivables and inventory. Having negative working capital can be a valuable strength because these businesses actually create cash as they expand.

Cash flow as profits, the second type of cash flow, is defined as net profits plus depreciation (after considering the appropriateness of the depreciation). Analysts should determine whether depreciation is too conservative, too aggressive, or simply appropriate. For example, Taekwang Industrial, a Korean synthetic fiber producer, completed a $450 million petrochemical facility that vertically integrated its basic business. In the first 2 1/2 years of operation, the company depreciated 75 percent of the facility, which has an economic life of 20–25 years. Clearly, Taekwang is taking a very aggressive stance on depreciation. Although some companies depreciate their assets too aggressively, sadly the great majority of companies in Asia depreciate too conservatively. Analysts and investors should consider how a company depreciates its assets and adjust profits accordingly.

The third and fourth types of cash flows—free cash flow and operating free cash flow—are similar. Free cash flow is EBITDA (earnings before interest, depreciation, and amortization) minus maintenance capital expenditures; operating free cash flow is EBITDA minus maintenance capital expenditures and maintenance working capital. Both types of cash flow are important; in fact, they get to the heart of the cash-generating nature of the business. Unfortunately, these cash flows tend to be volatile and difficult to analyze.

The final type of cash flow is the cash flow of the corporate structure. To understand this type of cash flow, consider two hypothetical companies. One company has a simple corporate structure that includes wholly owned subsidiaries. This company controls all the cash and can move cash efficiently between subsidiaries. The second company is a holding company that has a mix of subsidiaries that they own between 51 percent and 100 percent, associates that they own between 20 percent and 49 percent, and perhaps some joint ventures in China of undetermined ownership. Typically, cash exits the top holding company easily as new investments are undertaken, but cash enters slowly and then only through cash dividends. This situation leaves the top holding company chronically short of cash and long of debt, a dangerous combination. To deal with the inevitable cash shortages, this type of holding company resorts to a plethora of "rob Peter to pay Paul" strategies that include frequent capital raisings, many of which can be dilutive and disadvantageous to minority owners particularly in times of asset deflation. Consequently, the corporate structure must be closely examined.

In addition to the five types of cash flow, Asian companies mask as cash flow several items that have nothing in common with actual cash creation and must be discounted by analysts. These items include equity accounted profits that are not backed up by a 100 percent dividend payout ratio, capital raisings of both debt and equity, revaluations of assets, recording of nonrecurring items as ordinary income, and profits generated from the spin-off of subsidiaries.

Projections

Overlook Investments believes that projections are important, but making them is difficult in most environments. In this context, "projections" refers to forecasts for a period of three to five years, not for something as narrow as a company's earnings per share for the next quarter.

When making projections, analysts should keep four general principles in mind. First, analysts should recognize that all companies are different. Analysts should identify the factors that are important for the specific business in question and customize their projections and their historical analysis for each company.

Second, analysts should integrate the balance sheet, income statement, and statement of cash flows. This step is less of an issue today than in the past, but integrated financial statements are still critical in assisting analysts with gaining true insight into the specific business.

Third, analysts should obtain historical financial data for as long a period as possible. For example, analysts who have numbers for, say, a dozen years can have more confidence in making projections than if they only have a short company history. Over time, businesses go through cycles, and it is important to see how companies fare in their respective cycles. For example, at Overlook, we are analyzing a business in Hong Kong that has been public since 1987. For us, the ability to see 14 years of history is a real advantage. Most analysts make the mistake of evaluating only the past two or three years.

Finally, analysts should clearly specify the assumptions used to make projections. This enables them to revise their projections accurately if conditions warrant changing the underlying assumptions.

In summary, making good projections requires having a thorough knowledge about every aspect of the business. Obtaining complete data often requires repeat visits with companies. After going through this process, analysts should understand the cash flow dynamics of the business and should be able to evaluate the potential consistency of the business under different economic conditions and the sustainable return on equity.

Earnings Digests

At Overlook, we collect summary statistics from our earnings projections and put the information into our Earnings Digest, a management tool we have developed and refined over the past nine years. The Earnings Digest allows us to track the overall valuation characteristics of the portfolio and gives us an ability to improve our understanding of the valuation of the portfolio we own. We find this approach helps us not lose track of the valuation of the portfolio at the troughs of bear markets and at the peaks of bull markets. For example, a manager might say, "Well, my portfolio is not too bad. It is only 16 times earnings." In fact, it may have been 16 times earnings four months ago and the manager may have simply liked that story and kept it. Four months later, if the P/E is 23, the risk of overvaluation is greater.

The factual information that we collect on our companies includes size, capital structure, industry type, growth record, debt-to-equity ratio, historical growth rates, projected results, P/E, enterprise value (EV) to EBITDA, price-to-cash flow ratio, price-to-book-value ratio (P/BV), yield, ROE, and capital adequacy. We also make subjective judgments about the quality of the managers, the business, and our projections. We also include an entry that outlines the reasons for any recent changes in our projections so that we can easily reevaluate the critical parameters of the business.

The last step that we take is to aggregate this information for the portfolio as a whole on a dollar-weighted basis, including P/E, P/BV, ROE, EV/EBITDA, debt-to-equity ratio, yield, and growth rates. We do this so that we can determine the valuation of the whole portfolio and how it compares with our historical ranges.

We think the Earnings Digest permits efficient and effective monitoring of the portfolio because it provides for a process and a discipline. It allows us to isolate the absolute value in the portfolio and also helps us identify "red flags"—that is, which companies in the portfolio are stumbling. The Earnings Digest also allows us to monitor how current we are in terms of our company visits.[1] Over time, it helps us understand not only the accuracy of our own forecasting ability but the forecasting ability of certain businesses and certain CEOs.

---

[1] For further reading on the importance of company visits in the valuation process, see Zielinski (1998).

Enterprise Value and Operating Free Cash Flow

The investment world is moving toward cross-border standards in many aspects of financial analysis. The concept of enterprise value, or market capitalization, to EBITDA has contributed substantially to this change. Although the process has both advantages and disadvantages, such trade-offs should not dissuade analysts from examining stocks on this basis.

The process is particularly useful for international investing, particularly in Asia, for two reasons. First, EV/EBITDA helps to identify many failings of accounting policies. Second, it allows analysts to standardize analysis valuation across many markets.

Because EV/EBITDA has a bias in favor of cash-rich companies, it can help to identify investment opportunities. For example, at Overlook, we have been buying the stock of a Korean company that has net cash equal to about 130 percent of the share price. On an EV/EBITDA basis, it sells at about –0.75 times EV/EBITDA. On an EV/OFCF (operating free cash flow) basis, however, the valuation is about –0.37 times. The difference occurs because the company has been very successful at shrinking inventory and receivables and having almost no capital expenditures for the past 12 months. In other words, currently the company could pay out 132 percent of the share price in a dividend to all shareholders. If a leveraged buyout of the company was undertaken using 100 percent financing, the debt could be paid back in 128 days. So, the bias toward cash-rich companies is useful for identifying investment opportunities.

A disadvantage of the EV/EBITDA process is that it is not very useful for large companies and companies with complex structures, frequently Asia's large, indexed stocks. For holding companies, the process does not work because EBITDA numbers are often exaggerated and require additional analysis. The EV/EBITDA valuation method does not apply well to highly leveraged companies. Although many Korean companies are seemingly attractive based on an EV/EBITDA valuation, the method understates the risk of the substantial debt on the Korean balance sheets and overstates the EBITDA. Also, insufficient historical information is available on Asian companies to judge various EV/EBITDA and EV/OFCF figures in comparison with historical levels. In that regard, insufficient research, particularly on Asian companies, has been done by academicians on what determines an over- or undervalued company using EV/EBITDA.

Valuation

Valuation involves making decisions about estimates of risk and growth rates and the level of confidence in those estimates. At Overlook, we use a concept called "get close to cash," which means we require a meaningful cash return on the market capitalization of a stock we acquire. This cash return can either be paid out in cash dividends or retained by the business and reinvested at high rates of return. For example, we recently bought the stock of a company in Thailand, and because we expect to get our money out from dividends alone in only three years, we do not need the stock to go up.

We also use equations to help "de-emotionalize" the process of buying and selling securities. Specifically, we try to purchase stocks at P/Es of less than half the return on equity and less than half the long-term EPS growth rate. So, for a company growing at 20 percent with a 20 percent return on equity, we aim to buy the stock at less that 10 times EPS. In effect, we use the equations only as benchmarks, and they are not necessarily "the law."

We do not believe in discounted cash flow (DCF) analysis. How can an analyst accurately predict cash flows 20–30 years in the future? Such DCF forecasts are highly dependent on interest rates and discount rates. Recently, interest rates in Thailand went from 22 to 8 percent in nine months, and no analyst is likely to have used an 8 percent discount rate at the beginning of 1988. For analysts who believe in DCFs, an important concept is the duration of the cash flow. Mathematically, two companies may have an equal DCF value, but one may require large cash flows in the years 2010, 2011, and 2012 whereas the other may get the cash flow back in the next several years. Analysts who use DCF forecasts should not fall into the trap of buying too much blue sky.

Evaluation of Management

Evaluating management is an imperfect art, and no set of rules guarantees success. Our mandatory approach, however, is to make frequent company visits and to talk with managers, employees, suppliers, and customers. During these visits, we ask managers to identify specific events that are likely to occur in the company's future. When revisiting the company after three or four months, we ask managers about each item and determine whether the managers' views were correct or incorrect. This approach is a good way to identify talented managers.

The following characteristics are typical of successful managers in Asia:
- have a strong commitment to integrity,
- believe in progressive corporate governance,

- support the concept of transparency,
- go beyond the statutory requirements of the various stock exchanges,
- try to educate analysts and investors about their business,
- prefer to talk about next year's sales rather than last month's sales, and
- structurally align their interests with those of minority shareholders.

Another aspect of evaluating management is to evaluate the long-term corporate finance track record of all managers. Tigers typically do not change their stripes. If managers made decisions years ago that worked to the disadvantage of minority shareholders, they are likely to make poor decisions again, especially when under pressure.

Other items to watch out for when evaluating management:
- the managing director who brings out the entire management team on the first visit,
- the investor relations person who has a background in investment banking,
- deep discount rates on past issues of securities,
- related-party asset transactions,
- pyramid corporate structures,
- intergroup transactions,
- unproven second-generation management, and
- companies that lack professional managers.

Classic Ways to Destroy Value

Many companies in Asia have destroyed value, particularly during the period from January 1994 to December 1998. Analysts and investors should watch for several red flags that may signal the prospect of destroying value:

■ *Acquisition of assets from controlling shareholders.* The first classic way to destroy value is related-party transactions. In such transactions, a conflict of interest exists: a mismatch of knowledge and information between the insider seller and the outside buyer. Malaysian companies have led the way in acquisition of assets from shareholders. For example, the 1997 annual report of Berjaya Berhad disclosed 41 significant and related transactions, a list that continued for 11 pages.

■ *Unproductive investments by holding companies.* When looking at holding companies, analysts and investors should be extremely alert for items—such as low revenue per assets and weak corporate finance structures—that may lead to future cash drains, potential write-offs, and undisclosed debts. A good example is the Hong Kong holding company Guangdong Investments. Guangdong's unaudited figures for June 30, 1997, showed total assets of HK$19 billion. Revenue for the six months leading up to June 1997 was HK$3.4 billion, so annualized revenue was about HK$7 billion. In short, annual revenue was only about one-third of assets. After looking at such figures, I should not have been surprised when I visited one of Guangdong's companies, Guangdong Brewery. A year earlier, the company had completed a huge, new brewery at the cost of about HK$1.1 billion. At the time of my visit, the brewery had not produced a drop of beer or generated a dollar of revenue. Since then, Guangdong Investments itself ran into trouble in early 1999 and is undergoing debt restructuring.

■ *Excessive debt, off-balance-sheet debt, and debt guarantees.* Korean corporates lead the way in using excessive debt, off-balance-sheet debt, and debt guarantees. Usually, companies take such actions to hide bad news from investors. As a general rule, if an asset is great, it is usually in the private company, or if it is in the public company, it is not hidden off balance sheet. With off-balance-sheet items, the liabilities tend to be fixed and the value of the assets tend to be subjective. As a result, tremendous value destruction can occur without equity investors knowing what is happening.

One well-known example is Halla Group, a Korean second-tier *chaebol*. Although Halla had some good operating companies, its off-balance-sheet activity and debt guarantees got so severe that the company went bankrupt less than six months after the financial crisis hit Korea in late 1997.

■ *Fraud, lying, and unethical conduct.* Unfortunately, analysts and investors can do little to avoid fraud, lying, and unethical behavior. The only possible protection is to make frequent company visits and invest with people whom you feel you can trust. Generally, when a company is deteriorating, managers do not want to meet with analysts and investors. Stock exchanges and governments need to take strict action to correct this problem.

■ *Weak disclosure requirements by stock markets.* Another classic form of value destruction comes from weak disclosure requirements by the stock exchanges. Asian countries are trailing other markets on issues of transparency and disclosure, and surprisingly, Hong Kong trails behind most of Asia, with no requirement for disclosure of gross profit margin. I believe investors should not be called upon to evaluate a Hong Kong industrial company without knowing its gross profit margin. It is also very hard for honest managements to build a long-term track record with investors when investors do not see the gross profit margin. Not surprisingly, when bear markets roll through Hong Kong, controlling shareholders of industrial companies inevitably take advantage of poor disclosure to buy out minority investors at book value and two or three times earnings.

- *Poor auditing standards.* In Hong Kong, audited balance sheets are typically distributed once a year. If a company prefers, it can distribute its balance sheet four months after year end. At the end of April or in early May, the company distributes its December balance sheet and investors must wait another 12 months to receive another one. Delayed reporting opens up many opportunities for unethical activity, and this problem is particularly prevalent in public companies in Hong Kong.

On the other hand, companies in Thailand, which were maligned more than companies in any other Asian country in 1997–1998, provide quarterly income statements and balance sheets. Such information is timely and available on the Internet.

Although accounting policies tend to do a good job of telling how much toilet paper companies use, they do a poor job providing disclosure about the issues of real significance. Part of this failure rests with the stock exchanges, accounting policies, and poor government auditing standards.

- *Be a bank.* Another way to destroy value is to be a bank. Indonesian banks probably will set the standard on this way of destroying value. Managers of Asian banks seem to have a need to mislead analysts in terms of disclosing nonperforming loans and loan limits for single borrowers.

- *Mismatch of currencies and durations.* Another way to destroy significant value very quickly is by the mismatch of currencies. For example, funding long-term local currency investments with short-term U.S.-dollar-denominated liabilities can destroy incredible value in the event the home currency devalues and the local economy suffers an economic slump.

- *Unfunded pension liabilities.* Unfunded pension liabilities are a bigger problem than some analysts imagine. For example, a large company in Korea with 36,000 employees turned down an early-retirement request from 740 workers in May 1998 because such layoffs would have cost the company an incremental $200 million charge to the income statement. I calculated that properly accounting for the pension liability of the 36,000 employees would amount to about two-thirds of the company's share price, or about 2 percent of Korea's GNP. In practice, pension liabilities are just seeping into Asia, and Asian accounting policies on pension liabilities are extremely weak. Even when companies properly make the write-offs for the pension liabilities on the income statement, they often have not funded them.

- *Nonrecurring revenues and expenses.* Conceptually, taking out nonrecurring revenues and expenses is an easy process. In practice, many nonrecurring items are hidden in the normal income statement. So, analysts have to understand the business to determine whether nonrecurring items tend to exist.

- *Diversification outside the core area.* Diversification outside a company's core area may also destroy value. For example, CCT Telecom, which raised about $1.3 billion in an initial public offering in early 1998, developed a marketing and sales distribution network in China for telecommunication products. Because of a policy change by the Chinese central government, the project was unsuccessful. As a result, CCT Telecom used one-third of the IPO's proceeds to buy 51 percent of Cheerful Securities in Hong Kong, and Cheerful has had a less than cheerful record since its acquisition.

- *Repricing of share options.* Repricing of share options is a popular practice in Hong Kong. Some companies have repriced options not once but twice. Because they thought the bear market would end sooner than it did, these companies lowered the exercise price on an option once only to find later that they were too early, forcing them to lower the exercise price again.

- *Unaudited subsidiaries.* Another way to destroy value is to invest in companies with unaudited subsidiaries. Some places that have unaudited subsidiaries are the Cayman Islands, China, and Laos.

- *"Carve out approach" to raising capital.* State-owned enterprises (SOEs) in China developed the carve-out approach to raising capital. We call it "gain today and pay tomorrow." SOEs will carve out a revenue stream, keep the bulk of the expenses with the parent, float what looks like a profitable company at a nice P/E, and then slowly inject the expenses back in over time. For this reason alone, many stocks from China will continue to disappoint.

Success Factors in Investing

Being a successful investor in Asia is quite a challenge. At Overlook, we have identified several success factors that investors should keep in mind as they invest in Asian companies:

- *Build in a margin of safety.* Investors should not pay too dearly for stocks. As I mentioned earlier, investors should try to "get close to cash" by finding stocks that provide steady and meaningful dividends and significant amounts of free cash flow. Doing so will lessen the risks associated with overly optimistic projections or poor corporate practices.

- *Identify superior businesses.* Superior businesses are likely to prosper over the long run. These businesses do not necessarily have to be growth stocks. Value stocks can be superior businesses that are currently out of favor.

■ *Focus on the long-term horizon.* In the short run, markets may not recognize a company's potential or the quality of its management. Over time, however, stocks tend to move toward their true value.

■ *Focus on valuation.* Identifying the true value of a security is at the heart of security analysis. Using equations and benchmarks can reduce some of the emotional aspects associated with investing.

■ *Be dedicated to the art of investing.* Investing requires dedication and conviction. Chasing "hot" stocks and returns often suggests a lack of dedication and a tendency to go with the herd.

■ *Be able to stand alone.* Investors need to be able to stand alone with only their convictions as support. At times investing is a lonely business. Often, stocks drop after an initial purchase, increasing self-doubt and the fear of failure. The investor must realize their good fortune and average down.

■ *Consider smaller companies.* At Overlook, we believe in Roger Ibbotson's finding that smaller companies have rewarded investors—over long periods of time—better than large-capitalization stocks despite higher volatility.

■ *Have a sense of humor.* Bring your sense of humor; many of us would not have survived the events in Asia during the June 1997 to December 1998 period without it.

Conclusion

Finding economic reality in Asian earnings requires a combination of approaches. The first considerations are the tools, disciplines, and procedures to be used, with special emphasis on some unique challenges confronted by investors and analysts who work with Asia. Second, investors should be aware of the various ways in which many Asian companies have tended to destroy value, particularly the value of minority shareholders. Finally, investors need to know what factors are crucial to success for investing in Asian companies.

Practical Issues in Equity Analysis

Question and Answer Session

Richard H. Lawrence, Jr., CFA

Question: What types of questions do you ask managers during company visits that help you discover reality in earnings numbers, and can you easily tell when managers' responses are candid?

Lawrence: No simple answer to this question exists. If managers want to deceive you, they probably can. They can fool you once, maybe twice. By the third visit, however, you should be aware that discrepancies exist between what they are saying and what is actually happening.

The key is being prepared. You should show interest in and knowledge about the business and understand the manager's corporate finance track record so that you have a good feel for the type of manager with whom you are dealing. You should then follow up with more visits. Only through that process can you find out whether managers are telling the truth.

At Overlook, we ask many basic questions followed by specific questions. Often, we play dumb, particularly about future projections. For example, we might expect a company to make $200 million, but indicate a lower figure, say $130 million, to management. If the manager agrees with this assessment, we conclude that the company probably is going to make less than $130 million and maybe problems exist. On the other hand, if the manager says that the company is going to make at least $200 million, then our projections are probably reasonable. We typically believe that marketing directors are present during our visits because they are salespeople. They are more likely to mislead us than are the finance directors. So, meeting separately with marketing directors and finance directors is important.

Question: When do you expect your negative view about the restructuring of Korean companies to be reflected in the Korean stock market?

Lawrence: I expect the Korean stock market to decline. The problem that exists in Korea is based on the fact that Korean society is layered and does not easily change. Because Korean society is hierarchical, the country should have more trouble adjusting and restructuring its economy than South Asia and Southeast Asia will have. Korea also has more debt on a much broader scale than other Asian countries. On the positive side, the Korean people are excellent manufacturers, highly disciplined, and hard working; they have tremendous skills and determination to succeed. Companies that have their debt under control have a bright future because they should realize growth opportunities when available. Companies that have been stuck with too much debt are likely to restructure, which should lead to dilution.

The financial system is the weakest part of the Korean economy, and Korea has not maintained quality in banks. Because the bank loans and bankers lack quality, the write-offs have been gigantic. Korea has the same problem as everyone else in Asia—everyone has been asset lending. In periods of asset inflation, asset lending is a great business, but asset lending does not work in periods of asset and price deflation.

In Asia in general, banks have not done enough training. The governments do not have enough bank supervisors and are substantially behind in Korea and elsewhere in bank restructuring. At Overlook, we are negative on the banking business.

Question: Is the example of a small Korean company that had 130 percent of cash versus its share price an extremely rare case, or do you find a number of family-owned businesses in this situation?

Lawrence: Businesses with such strong balance sheets are rare, but not one in a thousand. Out of 500 public companies in Korea, fewer than 50 come close.

Question: Is the tremendous improvement in corporate reporting in Thailand a unique case, and do you have any observations on Asian companies in other countries that have shown considerable improvement?

Lawrence: Few Asian companies have pushed disclosure beyond that required by the stock markets. Although the Thai government officials have been slow in many areas, they have aggressively pushed reforms in corporate reporting. In Thailand, the tradition exists of providing quarterly income statements and balance sheets. Frequent disclosure, as opposed to getting only an annual balance sheet, makes a huge difference in analysts' understanding of a business. Thailand stands out as the best example of corporate reporting in Asia.

Other countries have moved in the direction of improved financial reporting. For example, companies in the Philippines issue quarterly accounts. Indonesia was moving in the right direction by offering quarterly balance sheets and income statements. Because of hyperinflation and the presence of off-balance-sheet hedge costs and gains, Indonesian accounts are difficult to decipher. But the Indonesian government recognized that the country relied on international investors and that it needed to provide these investors with quarterly balance sheets and income statements.

Question: Is determining the quality of earnings more difficult for particular industries or sectors than others?

Lawrence: Yes, determining quality of earnings is more difficult for large conglomerates, banks, finance companies, and joint venture companies. In fact, difficulty in determining the quality of earnings occurs when the capital structure is complex and, for example, when substantial income comes through associates or equity accounted earnings or when companies have substantial financial leverage. In general, good business people run simple businesses.

Question: What is Overlook's average holding period for an investment?

Lawrence: At Overlook, we have traditionally averaged about 20 percent turnover, which implies an average holding period of three to five years.

Question: What benchmarks does Overlook use in determining the size of its portfolio?

Lawrence: We try to hold 25 companies in the portfolio. We want 95 percent of the money in 25 companies and 50 percent of the money in 10 companies. At times, Overlook's portfolio has consisted of 30–33 companies because we have what we call an "incubator." When we come across a business that we like but have not thoroughly analyzed, we sometimes buy a few shares to make sure we learn more about the business. Generally, we have tended to have more concentration, having 50 percent of our money in 10 stocks. We do not believe that we can follow many companies at the same time.

Question: What is Overlook's view on shorting stocks?

Lawrence: Traditionally, Overlook has maintained a straight long portfolio. We are not enamored with the cash dynamics of shorting. We think that being long works to our advantage, especially in a part of the world that is generally growing. We do hedge our currencies if needed.

References

Abarbanell, Jeffery S., and Victor L. Bernard. 1992. "Tests of Analysts' Overreaction/Underreaction to Earnings Information as an Explanation for Anomalous Stock Price Behavior." *Journal of Finance* (July):1181–1207.

Atkinson, Thomas R. 1967. *Trends in Corporate Bond Quality*. New York: Columbia University Press.

Ball, Ray. 1978. "Anomalies in Relationships between Securities' Yields and Yield-Surrogates." *Journal of Financial Economics* (Spring/Fall):103–126.

Banz, Rolf W., and William J. Breen. 1986. "Sample-Dependent Results Using Accounting and Market Data: Some Evidence." *Journal of Finance* (September):779–793.

Barber, Brad, R. Lehavy, Maureen McNichols, and Bret Trueman. 1999. "Can Investors Profit from the Prophets?" Working paper, University of California at Davis.

Basu, Sanjoy. 1977. "Investment Performance of Common Stocks in Relation to Their Price–Earnings Ratios: A Test of the Efficient Market Hypothesis." *Journal of Finance* (June):663–682.

———. 1978. "The Effects of Earnings Yield on Assessments of the Association between Annual Accounting Income Numbers and Security Prices." *Accounting Review* (July):599–625.

———. 1983. "The Relationship between Earnings' Yield, Market Value, and Return for NYSE Common Stocks: Further Evidence." *Journal of Financial Economics* (June):129–156.

Berkshire Hathaway. 1995. *Annual Report*. Available online at www.berkshirehathaway.com/1995ar/1995ar.html

Bernard, V., and J.K. Thomas. 1989. "Post-Earnings-Announcement Drift: Delayed Price Response or Risk Premium?" *Journal of Accounting Research*, vol. 27 (supplement):1–36.

———. 1990. "Evidence that Stock Prices Do Not Fully Reflect the Implications of Current Earnings for Future Earnings." *Journal of Accounting and Economics*, vol. 13:305–340.

Bernstein, Richard. 1997. "An Analysis of EVA." *Merrill Lynch Quantitative Viewpoint*, December 19.

———. 1998. "An Analysis of EVA." *Merrill Lynch Quantitative Viewpoint*, February 3.

Biggs, Barton [1977]. "Investment Strategy." In *Classics: An Investor's Anthology*, edited by Charles D. Ellis and James R. Vertin. Homewood, IL: Business One Irwin, 1989:456–468.

Breen, William. 1968. "Low Price–Earnings Ratios and Industry Relatives." *Financial Analysts Journal* (July/August):125–127.

Buffett, Warren [1979]. "You Pay a Very High Price in the Stock Market for a Cheery Consensus." In *Classics: An Investor's Anthology*, edited by Charles D. Ellis and James R. Vertin. Homewood, IL: Business One Irwin, 1989:501–505.

——— [1987]. "Mr. Market, Investment Success and You." In *Classics II: Another Investor's Anthology*, edited by Charles D. Ellis and James R. Vertin. Homewood, IL: Business One Irwin, 1991:273–275.

——— [1989]. "Mistakes of the First Twenty-Five Years (A Condensed Version)." In *Classics: An Investor's Anthology*, edited by Charles D. Ellis and James R. Vertin. Homewood, IL: Business One Irwin, 1989:198–202.

Caginalp, Gunduz, David Porter, and Vernon Smith. Forthcoming 1999. "Overreactions, Momentum, Liquidity and Price Bubbles in Laboratory and Field Stock Markets." *Journal of Psychology and Financial Markets*.

Chopra, Vijay Kumar. 1998. "Why So Much Error in Analysts' Earnings Forecasts?" *Financial Analysts Journal* (November/December):35–42.

Cohen, Jerome B., Edward D. Zinbard, and Arthur Zeikel. 1973. *Investment Analysis and Portfolio Management*, rev. ed. Homewood, IL: R.D. Irwin.

Cohen, Jerome B., Edward D. Zinbarg, and Arthur Zeikel. 1982. Section 4 in *Investment Analysis and Portfolio Management*, 4th ed. Homewood, IL: Richard D. Irwin:337–467.

Davis, Henry [1962]. "An Investment Philosophy." In *Classics: An Investor's Anthology*, edited by Charles D. Ellis and James R. Vertin. Homewood, IL: Business One Irwin, 1989:323–338.

DeBondt, Werner F.M., and Richard H. Thaler. 1985. "Does the Stock Market Overreact?" *Journal of Finance* (July):793–805.

———. 1987. "Further Evidence on Investor Overreaction and Stock Market Seasonality." *Journal of Finance* (July):557–580.

Dodd, David L., and Benjamin Graham. 1934. *Security Analysis*. New York: McGraw-Hill.

Dreman, David. 1977. *Psychology and the Stock Market*. New York: AMACOM.

———. 1979. *Contrarian Investment Strategy*. New York: Random House.

———. 1982. *The New Contrarian Investment Strategy*. New York: Random House.

———. 1990. "Getting Ready for the Rebound." *Forbes* (July 23):376.

———. 1998. *Contrarian Investment Strategies: The Next Generation*. New York: Simon & Schuster.

Dreman, David N., and Michael A. Berry. 1995a. "Analyst Forecasting Errors and Their Implications for Security Analysis." *Financial Analysts Journal* (May/June):30–41.

Dreman, David, and Michael Berry. 1995b. "Overreaction, Underreaction, and the Low-P/E Effect." *Financial Analysts Journal* (July/August):21–30.

Dreman, David, and Eric Lufkin. 1997. "Do Contrarian Strategies Work within Industries?" *Journal of Investing* (Fall):7–29.

———. Forthcoming 1999. "Investor Overreaction: Evidence That Its Basis Is Psychological." *Journal of Psychology and Financial Markets*.

Ehrbar, Al. 1998. *EVA: The Real Key to Creating Wealth*. New York: John Wiley & Sons.

Ellis, Charles D. 1982. "Ben Graham: Ideas as Mementos." *Financial Analysts Journal* (July/August):41–42, 44–48.

Fama, Eugene F., and Kenneth R. French. 1992. "The Cross-Section of Expected Stock Returns." *Journal of Finance* (June):427–466.

———. 1995. "Size and Book-to-Market Factors in Earnings and Returns." *Journal of Finance* (March):131–155.

———. 1996. "Multifactor Explanations of Asset Pricing Anomalies." *Journal of Finance* (March):55–84.

Fisher, Philip [1958]. "What to Buy—The Fifteen Points to Look for in a Common Stock." In *Classics: An Investor's Anthology*, edited by Charles D. Ellis and James R. Vertin. Homewood, IL: Business One Irwin, 1989:230–252.

Graham, Benjamin. 1949. *The Intelligent Investor: A Book of Practical Advice*. New York: Harper.

———. 1985. Chapters 17–18 and Chapter 20 in *The Intelligent Investor*, 4th ed. New York: Harper Collins.

Grossman, S.J., and J.E. Stiglitz. 1980. "On the Impossibility of Informationally Efficient Markets." *American Economic Review* (June).

Hickman, W. Braddock. 1958. *Corporate Bond Quality and Investor Experience*. Princeton, NJ: Princeton University Press for National Bureau of Economic Research.

Ibbotson, Roger. 1989. "The Long-Term Perspective." In *Stocks, Bonds, Bills and Inflation: Historical Returns (1926-1987)*. Chicago, IL: Dow Jones–Irwin.

Ikenberry, David L., Graeme Rankine, and Earl K. Stice. 1996. "What Do Stock Splits Really Signal?" *Journal of Financial and Quantitative Analysis* (September):357–375.

Investment Company Institute. 1996. "Shareholder Assessment of Risk Disclosure Methods." Research report (Spring):1–39.

Jenrette, Richard [1966]. "Portfolio Management: Seven Ways to Improve Performance." In *Classics: An Investor's Anthology*, edited by Charles D. Ellis and James R. Vertin. Homewood, IL: Business One Irwin, 1989:382–391.

Kahneman, Daniel, and Dan Lovallo. 1993. "Timid Choices and Bold Forecasts: A Cognitive Perspective on Risk Taking." *Management Science* (January):17–31.

Kahneman, Daniel, and Amos Tversky [1973]. "On the Psychology of Prediction." In *Judgement under Uncertainty: Heuristics and Biases*, edited by Daniel Kahneman, Paul Slovic, and Amos Tversky. New York: Cambridge University Press, 1982:48–68.

Kahneman, Daniel, Paul Slovic, and Amos Tversky, eds. 1982. *Judgment under Uncertainty: Heuristics and Biases*. New York: Cambridge University Press.

Kaplan, Paul D. and Laurence B. Siegel. 1994. "Portfolio Theory Is Alive and Well." *Journal of Investing* (Fall):18–22.

Kringman, Laurie, Wayne Shaw, and Kent L. Womack. Forthcoming 2000. "Why Do Firms Switch Underwriters?" *Journal of Financial Economics*.

Lakonishok, Josef, Andrei Shleifer, and Robert Vishny. 1994. "Contrarian Investment, Extrapolations, and Risk." *Journal of Finance* (December):1541–78.

Lev, Baruch, and Theodore Sougiannis. 1996. "The Capitalization, Amortization, and Value-Relevance of R&D." *Journal of Accounting & Economics* (February):107–138.

Loughran, Tim, and Jay Ritter. 1995. "The New Issues Puzzle." *Journal of Finance* (March):23–51.

———. 1996. "Long-Term Market Overreaction: The Effect of Low-Priced Stocks." *Journal of Finance* (December):1959–70.

———. 1997. "The Operating Performance of Firms Conducting Seasoned Equity Offerings." *Journal of Finance* (December):1832–50.

Lynch, Aaron. 1996. *Thought Contagion: How Beliefs Spread through Society*. New York: Basic Books.

———. Forthcoming 1999. "Thought Contagion in the Stock Market." *Journal of Psychology and Financial Markets*.

Lynch, Peter. 1989. *One Up on Wall Street*. New York: Simon & Schuster.

Madden, Bartley J. 1999. *CFROI Valuation: A Total System Approach to Valuing the Firm*. New York: Butterworth-Heinemann.

Marine Midland Bank. 1968. Untitled research report.

Markowitz, Harry. *Portfolio Selection: Efficient Diversification of Investments*. New York: John Wiley & Sons.

McWilliams, J.D. 1966. "Prices and Price/Earnings Ratios." *Financial Analysts Journal* (May/June):137–142.

Michaely, Roni, and Kent L. Womack. 1999. "Conflicts of Interests and the Credibility of Underwriter Analysts Recommendations." *Review of Financial Studies* (Winter):653–686.

Michaely, Roni, Richard Thaler, and Kent Womack. 1995. "Price Reactions to Dividend Initiations and Omissions: Overreaction or Drift?" *Journal of Finance* (June):573–608.

Miller, P.F., and E.R. Widmann. 1966. "Price Performance Outlook for High and Low P/E Stocks." 1996 Stock and Bond Issue, *Commercial and Financial Chronicle* (September 29):26–28.

Naess, Ragnar D. [1963]. "The Enigma of Investment Management." In *Classics: An Investor's Anthology*, edited by Charles D. Ellis and James R. Vertin. Homewood, IL: Business One Irwin, 1989:405–411.

Nicholson, Francis. 1960. "Price–Earnings Ratio." *Financial Analysts Journal* (July/August):43–45.

———. 1968. "Price–Earnings Ratios in Relation to Investment Results." *Financial Analysts Journal* (January/February):105–109.

Olsen, Robert A. 1997. "Investment Risk: The Experts' Perspective." *Financial Analysts Journal* (March/April):62–66.

Payne, John. 1973. "Alternative Approaches to Decision Making under Risk: Moments vs. Risk Dimensions." *Psychological Bulletin*, vol. 80, no. 6 (December):439–453.

Porter, David P., and Vernon L. Smith. 1994. "Stock Market Bubbles in the Laboratory." *Applied Mathematical Finance*, vol. 1:111–27.

Rappaport, Alfred. 1986. *Creating Shareholder Value*. New York: Free Press.

Reinganum, Marc R. 1981. "Misspecification of Capital Asset Pricing: Empirical Anomalies Based on Earnings Yields and Market Values." *Journal of Financial Economics* (March):19–46.

Ritter, Jay. 1991. "The Long-Run Performance of Initial Public Offerings." *Journal of Finance* (March):3–28.

Roll, Richard. 1992. "Industrial Structure and the Comparative Behavior of International Stock Market Indexes." *Journal of Finance* (March):3–42.

Shiller, Robert. 1981. "Do Stock Prices Move Too Much to Be Justified by Subsequent Changes in Dividends?" *American Economic Review*, vol. 71:421–436.

Smith, Vernon L. 1992. "The Robustness of Bubbles and Crashes in Experimental Stock Markets." In *Nonlinear Dynamics and Evolutionary Economics*, edited by I. Prigogine, R. Day, and P. Chan. Oxford, U.K.: Oxford University Press.

Smith, Vernon L., Gerry L. Suchanek, and Arlington W. Williams. 1988. "Bubbles, Crashes, and Endogenous Expectations in Experimental Spot Asset Markets." *Econometrica* (September):1119–51.

Stickel, Scott E. 1992. "Reputation and Performance among Security Analysts." *Journal of Finance* (December):1811–36.

Tighe, Laurence G. [1940]. "The Yale Plan." In *Classics II: Another Investor's Anthology*, edited by Charles D. Ellis and James R. Vertin. Homewood, IL: Business One Irwin, 1991:282–286.

Train, John. 1989. Chapter 7 in *The New Money Managers*. New York: Harper Collins.

Tversky, Amos, and Daniel Kahneman [1974]. "Judgment under Uncertainty: Heuristics and Biases." In *Judgment under Uncertainty: Heuristics and Biases*, edited by Daniel Kahneman, Paul Slovic, and Amos Tversky. New York: Cambridge University Press, 1982:3–20.

Womack, Kent L. 1996. "Do Brokerage Analysts' Recommendations Have Investment Value?" *Journal of Finance* (March):137–167.

Zeikel, Arthur [1975]. "On the Threat of Change." In *Classics: An Investor's Anthology*, edited by Charles D. Ellis and James R. Vertin. Homewood, IL: Business One Irwin, 1989:660–670.

Zielinski, Robert G. 1998. "Research Techniques in Asian Markets." In *Asian Equity Investing*. Charlottesville, VA: AIMR:17–26.

Selected Publications

AIMR

AIMR Performance Presentation Standards Handbook, 2nd edition, 1997

Alternative Investing, 1998

Asian Equity Investing, 1998

Asset Allocation in a Changing World, 1998

Credit Analysis Around the World, 1998

Currency Risk in Investment Portfolios, 1999

Derivatives in Portfolio Management, 1998

Equity Research and Valuation Techniques, 1998

Frontiers in Credit-Risk Analysis, 1999

The Future of Investment Management, 1998

Investment Counseling for Private Clients, 1999

Risk Management: Principles and Practices, 1999

Standards of Practice Handbook, 8th ed., 1999

Research Foundation

Company Performance and Measures of Value Added, 1996
by Pamela P. Peterson, CFA, and David R. Peterson

Controlling Misfit Risk in Multiple-Manager Investment Programs, 1998
by Jeffery V. Bailey, CFA, and David E. Tierney

Country Risk in Global Financial Management, 1997
by Claude B. Erb, CFA, Campbell R. Harvey, and Tadas E. Viskanta

Economic Foundations of Capital Market Returns, 1997
by Brian D. Singer, CFA, and Kevin Terhaar, CFA

Interest Rate Modeling and the Risk Premiums in Interest Rate Swaps, 1997
by Robert Brooks, CFA

The International Equity Commitment, 1998
by Stephen A. Gorman

Investment Styles, Market Anomalies, and Global Stock Selection, 1999
by Richard O. Michaud

Long-Range Forecasting, 1999
by William S. Gray, CFA

Sales-Driven Franchise Value, 1997
by Martin L. Leibowitz

U.S. POSTAL SERVICE
STATEMENT OF OWNERSHIP, MANAGEMENT, AND CIRCULATION
(Required by 39 U.S.C. 3685)

1. Title of Publication: *AIMR Continuing Education*
2. Publication No.: 013-739
3. Filing Date: February 21, 2000
4. Issue Frequency: Four Times a Year
5. Number of Issues Published Annually: 4
6. Annual Subscription Price: US$100
7. Complete Mailing Address of Known Office of Publication (Street, City, County, State, and Zip+4) (Not Printer)
   Association for Investment Management and Research
   P.O. Box 3668, Charlottesville, VA 22903-0668
8. Complete Mailing Address of Headquarters or General Business Office of Publisher (Not Printer)
   Association for Investment Management and Research
   P.O. Box 3668, Charlottesville, VA 22903-0668
9. Full Names and Complete Mailing Addresses of Publisher, Editor, and Managing Editor (Do Not Leave Blank)
   Publisher (Name and Complete Mailing Address)
       Jaynee M. Dudley, AIMR, P.O. Box 3668, Charlottesville, VA 22903-0668
   Editor (Name and Complete Mailing Address)
       Katrina F. Sherrerd, AIMR, P.O. Box 3668, Charlottesville, VA 22903-0668
   Managing Editor (Name and Complete Mailing Address)
       Bette Collins, AIMR, P.O. Box 3668, Charlottesville, VA 22903-0688
10. Owner (If owned by a corporation, its name and address must be stated and also immediately thereafter the names and addresses of stockholders owning or holding 1 percent or more of the total amount of stock. If not owned by a corporation, the names and addresses of the individual owners must be given. If owned by a partnership or other unincorporated firm, its name and address as well as that of each individual must be given. If the publication is published by a nonprofit organization, its name and address must be given.) (Do Not Leave Blank)
    Association for Investment Management and Research, P.O. Box 3668,
    Charlottesville, VA 22903-0668
11. Known Bondholders, Mortgagees, and Other Security Holders Owning or Holding 1 Percent or More of Total Amount of Bonds, Mortgages or Other Securities. If none, check here. ✔ None.
12. For completion by nonprofit organization authorized to mail at special rates. The purpose, function, and nonprofit status of the organization and the exempt status for Federal income tax purposes: (Check one.)

    ✔ Has Not Changed During Preceding 12 Months   Has Changed During Preceding 12 Months (If changed, publisher must submit explanation of change with this statement.)

13. Publication Name: *AIMR Continuing Education*
14. Issue Date for Circulation Data Below: January/February 1999 through November/December 1999

15. Extent and Nature of Circulation	Average No. Copies Each Issue During Preceding 12 Months	Actual No. of Copies of Single Issue Published Nearest to Filing Date
a. Total No. Copies (Net Press Run)	34,153	34,650
b. Paid and/or Requested Circulation		
1. Sales Through Dealers and Carriers, Street Vendors, and Counter Sales		
2. Paid or Requested Mail Subscriptions	28,843	27,325
c. Total Paid and/or Requested Circulation (sum of 15b(1) and 15b(2))	28,843	27,325
d. Free Distribution by Mail, Samples, Complimentary, and Other Free	188	200
e. Free Distribution Outside the Mail		
f. Total Distribution (sum of 15d and 15e)	188	200
g. Total Distribution (sum of 15c and 15f)	29,031	27,525
h. Copies Not Distributed		
1. Office Use, Leftovers, Spoiled	5,122	7,125
2. Returns from News Agents		
i. Total (sum of 15g, 15h(1), and 15h(2))	34,153	34,650
Percent Paid and/or Requested Circulation (15c/15g × 100)	100	100

16. This Statement of Ownership will be printed in the 2000, vol. 1, no. 1 issue of this publication.
17. I certify that all information furnished on this form is true and complete. I understand that anyone who furnishes false or misleading information on this form or who omits material or information requested on the form may be subject to criminal sanctions (including fines and imprisonment) and/or civil sanctions (including multiple damages and civil penalties).

Signature and Title of Editor, Publisher, Business Manager, or Owner
Jaynee Dudley, Publisher